The Bishop

The Story of A. A. Leiske and the
Unique Telecast—"The American
Religious Town Hall Meeting"

Horace J. Shaw

Pacific Press Publishing Association
Mountain View, California
Oshawa, Ontario

Cover illustration by Sue Rother

Library of Congress Cataloging in Publication Data

Shaw, Horace John, 1909-
  The bishop.

  1. Leiske, Albert A., 1901-   . 2. American Religious Town Hall
Meeting (Television program) 3. Television in religion—United
States. 4. Evangelists—United States—Biography. I. Title.
BV3785.L36S5   286.7'3 [B]   81-11191
ISBN 0-8163-0444-0   AACR2

Contents

Preface:
What Manner of Man?

Five months of North Dakota winter had begun to give way to early signs of spring in late March of 1901. Snow still covered the fields, but the drifts along the country roads had melted down to fence-post level. Sounds carried far on the crisp morning air, and early risers could hear the lowing of their neighbors' cattle miles away.

People passing by the farmhouse of Gottlieb and Elisabeth Leiske, six miles from the little town of Heaton, noticed an unusual amount of activity the morning of March 27. Tracks in the snow indicated considerable traffic in and out during the night. Soon the news spread from farm to farm that a new baby boy had been born to this family, their eighth child.

Albert, they christened him, little realizing that this name with the title "Bishop" attached to it later would some day be known to millions through a unique television ministry. To Albert's parents this new arrival merely promised additional help by and by on the farm.

Albert did indeed do his full share of work on the farm. But passing time began to unfold a story of this boy so different from his brothers and sisters. It became evident that he, even at nine years of age, had been marked for an exceptional and influential role in God's service. For one thing, he had an unusual gift for speaking. Also a remarkable capacity to sympathize.

Poverty, illness, and hard work during Albert's growing-up years built stern qualities into his character that future challenges would demand. Also his mother's godly influence, plus the religious environment of a Christian home, shaped his destiny, leading him to choices in his teen years to follow God's plan for his life.

Out of this interesting mix of heritage and background emerges a rare portrayal. What kind of man did the boy become? Bold and captivating strokes show up in the picture, revealing an uncommon chemistry in Albert's personality. "He could chew you up and spit you out," remembers one admirer, "yet be most understanding and compassionate."

We see him as a pulpiteer and puppeteer, student and showman, the grave one and the humorist. "A well-mannered, good-natured hurricane," one acquaintance described him. Fifteen years of tent pitching and preaching fostered both the Billy Sunday and the P. T. Barnum in him.

To get his crowds he had to do strategic planning. He explored by the trial-and-error method. He had to consider a whole spectrum of factors: good location, catchy ads, musical features, special attractions, intriguing topics, fearless presentations, up-the-sleeve surprises, and financial resources.

In handling all these details, the motivation had to be spiritual. The constant concern that kept holy zeal burning in Albert's heart stemmed from his longing to save souls for God's kingdom. It came to be a pressure-cooker existence: Find the people, deliver the summons, get the verdict. Baptize and organize. Build and move on. Then again pitch, preach, baptize, build, and move on.

And again, time after time, Albert A. Leiske tent-and-tabernacle-stormed through North Dakota, Missouri, Kansas, Nebraska, Texas, and Colorado during the twenties, the thirties, and the forties, setting a pace few could endure.

The next three decades, the fifties through the seventies,

Albert Leiske entered the era of an expanded ministry due largely to a dream that came to him while pastoring the Seventh-day Adventist church in St. Paul, Minnesota. In this lifelike dream, he saw himself leading ministers of other denominations in open discussions on television. The dream made such an impact on him that he awoke at two o'clock the morning of December 1, 1952, and wrote out the charter for what became by the end of the month the American Religious Town Hall Meeting, Inc.

Landmark decisions followed at the December 5 and 30 agreements by the five prospective panelists and several participating witnesses. These decisions involved selecting A. A. Leiske as moderator and granting him the title of Bishop.

Enthusiasm ran high at the first telecast of the "American Religious Town Hall Meeting," January 10, 1953, as the panelists of five denominations met in the studio of WCCO-TV in Minneapolis. And it has run high ever since.

In a "super-reach," in mid-August 1954, Leiske visited the ABC network in Chicago with plans to go national. A week later, August 21, he had the panelists paying their own train fares to Chicago with an overnight stop at the LaSalle Hotel plus a daytime schedule of half-hour "takes" by kinescope in the Civic Theater. Soon seventy-five stations began airing the Town Hall programs.

But costs began to mount faster than expected. That fall in Washington, D.C., the General Conference of the Seventh-day Adventist Church gave moral support to the interfaith broadcast operations. By the spring of 1955, however, they had become leery of those snowballing expenses. Donations dwindled. Total assets dipped to only $32 while indebtedness rose to $8000. Fearing a day of reckoning, the local SDA Minnesota conference (with Albert Leiske on its payroll) gave this ultimatum: "Be solvent by July 31 or go off the air."

To this directive the St. Paul Adventist pastor agreed.

The project should be operated on a pay-as-you-go basis. This policy he had followed as a matter of course in his many evangelistic campaigns. Right then Albert and Mae Leiske committed themselves to an Abraham-like faith: "God will provide." But how?

Then the miracle of the cemetery plots took place.

How did Albert Leiske react to the financial stricture and embarrassment he barely escaped? He couldn't count on conference leaders to back him in any program of expansion. To be sure that the TV wagon would be able to go forward whenever there would be an opportunity, he envisioned the need for a freestanding, separate organization, fully wheeled and ready to go, uphill or down, ready to round the curves at any admissible speed.

He discovered, in studying the Minnesota state law, the ways and means for effecting such an organization. He could incorporate under the Minnesota Non-Profit Corporation Act of 1951. With the advice and assistance of his fellow clergy panelists (Ira Allen, a Methodist, and Ansgar Nelson, a Lutheran) a Town Hall Corporation became a legal entity on August 8, 1955.

In the organization A. A. Leiske, as founder, holds 51 percent of the stock; and as the legal head officer he carries the deciding vote in all matters of the Town Hall operations. Thus no longer did the preacher-evangelist now turned moderator and corporate head need to await church or conference permission to undertake new projects. Now himself the principal and responsible officer, to act with the assistance and advice of fellow board members, he could move ahead on his own. This new corporation would now decide when to apply the brakes and when the accelerator. The corporation was now autonomous, and he sat in the driver's seat.

This new nonprofit corporation could now do such things as sell or mortgage cemetery lots. "Pay-up or fold-up" deadlines could no more be drawn against them. The organization now had power to generate its own capital, to hold, to sell, or to reinvest.

Ralph Waldo Emerson once observed, "An institution is but the lengthened shadow of a man." Thus viewed, the American Religious Town Hall Meetings, Inc. stands as the lengthened shadow of Bishop Albert A. Leiske. It holds millions of dollars of property in nursing and residence homes and hospitals, with thousands of patrons, served by hundreds of dedicated administrators and employees.

And all this vast enterprise for just one great purpose—to beam brotherhood to the nations on television. The "tension barrier" between churches needed to be broken and intolerance abolished. Bishop Leiske saw himself in a dream appointed by God to this role, joining with men of differing faiths in a sweeping presentation of the gospel to the millions. Motivated by what he saw and spurred by concepts forming in his mind since boyhood, he rose to the challenge and led out in the creation of the "American Religious Town Hall Meeting," eventually structuring a corporation to sustain it.

And now the fantastic story as it unfolds!

Acknowledgments

"You must write a book on Albert," Mae Leiske said. She pressed her plea by phone, by letter, and face-to-face. The task began in September 1978. An appeal was made to friends and associates to share their reminiscences. Within a month scores of letters and taped conversations filled a bulging four-inch three-ring notebook of responses that Mae reviewed with great satisfaction. Then the unexpected. In a matter of days Mae, the beloved "Mother Superior," was summoned to surgery in a Dallas hospital but succumed two days later. What preceded and followed that fateful October is sketched in the following pages.

I wish to express my gratitude to those scores of respondents who provided hitherto unknown glimpses of the Bishop and his paradigm of traits that often inspire and at times bemuse and baffle a biographer. I wish to acknowledge a debt I owe my esteemed mentor, Dr. Kenneth G. Hance, for the overall schema of outline and voluntary appraisal and positioning of each respondent's reply for source references.

Any reader knows that telling a story is a skill apart from the craft of writing topically or historically. My genuine thanks goes to Herbert E. Douglass, Editor-in-chief of English publications at the Pacific Press, for recommending his predecessor, T. R. (Ted) Torkelson, as collaborator and consultant. Ted's ability to select, to show-and-tell, has done more than anything else to pass along the light from the Bishop's torch. Ted and I both wish to express our thanks to Norma Youngberg, author of forty storybooks and dean of Adventist storywriters for her counsel. A salute, not just a thankful wave of the hand, goes to my longtime friend and associate in public relations and alumni affairs at Andrews Univeristy, Opal Hoover Young, former editor of *Focus*. Without a beg, while weekending with my family, Opal checked the manuscript for further correction. In addition sincere thanks goes to our Town Hall administrators, Robert W. Leiske, president, and Delano F. Forsberg, vice-president, for releasing their secretaries to do the transcription and typing. For revisionary assistance in typing the final manuscript draft, Wana Schneider Leiske rates a teacher's exceptional grade of A + for excellence.

And what more shall I offer but a heart full of love to my dear, devoted Dorothy, whose ready ear and ever-cheerful smile inevitably brought vigor to re-steam when the drive wheels seemed locked at dead center.

If you, dear reader, can see through human fears and foibles to the triumph of the overriding providence of the divine Maker of Men, then you have discerned the intent of this member of the "Planning Department," who has watched for thirty years a dreamer's dream develop.

Horace J. Shaw

Foreword

Bishop A. A. Leiske is known throughout the nation in both church circles and the business world. He is talented in many areas of activity. He has been successful as a church pastor and as a public evangelist, both in rural communities and in large cities. In addition, he has been unusually successful as the organizer and moderator of the "American Religious Town Hall Meeting," a nationally known televised discussion program that is unique in its purpose, scope, subject matter, and interfaith outreach. And he is equally successful as the organizer, developer, and chief executive officer of a multimillion-dollar organization which is outstanding in the health-care field.

Born of immigrant parents and brought up on a farm in rugged North Dakota, Bishop Leiske developed himself through hard work, academy and college training, and extensive practice in public speaking, preaching, and church and business administration. His strong character, religious faith and knowledge, and social consciousness, together with a personality marked by enthusiasm and friendly outreach, make a most interesting story.

It is, indeed, appropriate that Dr. Horace J. Shaw should undertake the Bishop's biography. More than thirty years of acquaintanceship with A. A. Leiske and twenty-seven years of close association with the organization and a deep interest in its goals and the subject matter of its discussions, together with academic preparation, provide a basis for a discerning understanding and scholarly approach and treatment of the material.

Bishop Leiske and Dr. Shaw share several areas of mutual interest and concern—strong attachment to the church, involvement in the Christian ministry, and personal interests that have made for strong ties over the years. The close associations with the American Religious Town Hall Meeting, Inc., and the telecasts, which went nationwide in 1953, have involved Dr. Shaw's serving as program announcer and consultant—perhaps as deep involvement as that of any person other than Bishop Leiske himself.

Dr. Shaw also brings to this study valid academic credentials and experiences for this project. His college undergraduate field of concentration was religion; the focus of his M.A. program was speech, radio, and television; and his Ph.D. program concentrated in the field of rhetoric and public address, including attention to the theories and practices of oral communication in public speaking, argumentation, persuasion, preaching, and group discussion. In addition, his doctoral dissertation provided him with experiences in the study of public speaker-preacher and investigations into biography, history, religion, and a variety of rhetorical practices.

The Bishop is, indeed, a study of a significant person and an equally significant institution presented by a person with unique credentials in terms of interest, knowledge, and understanding regarding the subject and equally unique and significant credentials to perform this task.

KENNETH G. HANCE, PH.D.
Emeritus Professor, Michigan State University
Adjunct Professor, Andrews University
Past President of the Speech Association of America

Chose the Right Parents

"That boy of yours is going to be an orator and a public speaker someday." Albert Leiske, sixteen-year-old son of a North Dakota farmer, overheard the banker in his hometown of Heaton make this remark to his father, Gottlieb Leiske, one evening. Were they talking about him?

Albert had just given a speech at a patriotic meeting in the town square and had received a thunderous applause. Still in grade school at the time, he felt like a rookie batter who has just scored a home run for his team.

That year, 1917, marked the third year of World War I, and the country needed money from the sale of bonds. In keeping with the mood of the times, Albert had titled his talk "America Will Survive Through Sacrifice."

This country lad, next to the youngest in a family of nine children, observed the gleam in his father's eye as the banker kept talking. It seemed to him that from then on his father began thinking big thoughts for him.

"What are your plans for the future?" he asked Albert a day or so later back on the farm. Albert tried to read his father's mind, wondering if the conversation with the banker had prompted the question.

Well, what *are* my plans? Albert thought to himself later. His father had not pressed for a reply at the time, but he had started Albert's brain cells churning out possible ideas. Maybe he *was* supposed to be an orator. He remembered hearing his mother say more than once that if he ever died "they would have to sew his mouth shut to keep him from talking in his coffin." And the kids at school said he had the "gift of gab" like no one they had ever heard before.

"You could never win an argument with him," declared one of his classmates; "he was so good at debating." Even with his father, who could as effectively turn off something he didn't want to hear as if he wore a hearing aid, Albert had a way of getting through and winning his point. Once at age thirteen he got excited about buying a white nanny goat with harness and wagon. The big problem, as he analyzed it, had to do with raising the money and with getting his father's consent. He put up a terrific argument and talked his father into letting him buy it.

As time went on, Albert felt he could detect in little things his parents said and did that they had ambitions for him different from what they apparently had had for the older children. He had watched his five brothers grow to manhood and leave home to start farming on their own or go into business. And his two older sisters had married farmers. He had observed that in no case had they gone on with their education beyond the local grade school. As Albert finished the eighth grade at age seventeen, he faced one of the big decisions of his life—to go on to high school and maybe to college, or to leave school and continue farming as his brothers had done.

He loved the farm. The smells of freshly plowed fields in spring and the new-mown hay in summer held a special attraction for him. The sound of a cow bawling for her calf seemed like music to him. And the prairie sunsets stimulated his thoughts to high ideals. He took his place early behind a five-horse team on a gangplow, working along with his brothers getting the fields ready for the wheat crop. He used to say to himself, "They may get this hick out of the country, but they'll never get the country out of this hick."

Albert recalls how the meadowlarks meant something special to him as a boy and deepened his love for the out-of-doors. "We had very few birds where I lived," he says, "but we had meadowlarks sing for us every spring." Even yet he never hears that clear tuneful call without feeling a sense of nostalgia and a desire to come closer to God. "Those birds made a tremendous impact on me to dedicate my life to helping people and to serving God."

This North Dakota farm boy, later turned preacher, doesn't remember just when his thinking began to take a religious turn. But he now believes that those early years among the things of nature had a lot to do with it. A vastly greater influence, however, he quickly concedes, stemmed from his parents' attitudes about God and the Bible, and about life in general, especially his mother's part in exerting this influence.

He of course didn't choose his parents, but he recognizes God's providence in choosing for him parents who had sterling qualities of steadfastness and courage and who feared God and lived by principle. Traits that rubbed off onto him from daily association with them during his formative years, and the genes they transmitted to him, he sees as determining factors in shaping what later became his unique and rewarding career for God.

Young Albert had been fascinated by stories of his family in the old country and read every book he could find on Russia of that period. As he read accounts of suffering and hardships, he relived in imagination what his grandparents and his own parents had endured and was deeply impressed.

Albert often heard his father talk about his own boyhood and youth in Russia. Two generations earlier his father's grandparents, along with other families from Poland and Germany, had responded to an appeal made by Catherine the Great of Russia for skilled farmers to move into the Crimea and develop the country. "She promised liberty and freedom of worship to these immigrants," Albert's father had recounted. "But after Catherine's death, this attitude completely changed."

Even though the Russian government had promised these immigrant farmers religious freedom, after some years the government reneged on the agreement. Dissent from the state church (Russian Orthodox) came under severe censorship, with any deviation from the prescribed form of worship relentlessly crushed out.

One of the history books told about a Baptist preacher named Mr. Schiewe, who for baptizing more than four hundred converts, had to pay a great price. Government authorities imprisoned him seven times and finally banished him into exile, never to see his wife and children again. Thousands of Baptists suffered banishment to Siberia, the history books said, their only crime being that they worshiped in a way different from the church established by law and that they dared to share their faith with their neighbors.

Albert had learned from listening to his father that the Leiske family, too, had suffered persecution in Russia because of their Baptist beliefs and religious practices. Once the police suddenly broke into the home where they and a few other families had gathered to study the Scriptures. Evidently someone had spied on them. The authorities slapped a stiff fine on the young couple in whose home the meeting had taken place.

On another occasion soldiers on horses surrounded the home where the believers had assembled to worship. The penalty this time fell on every male in the group, not just on the couple who owned the house. All the men had to serve time as prisoners in a dungeon.

As Albert relived these experiences, he developed a deep appreciation for his father and mother and for their devotion to God and their courage to stand firm against such great odds. He admired their venturesome spirit too, which led them in 1885 to cut their ties with their homeland and migrate to the United States. In Albert's estimation this was a bold move requiring much faith and backbone.

The deep feelings stirred up in Albert's soul he could not

interpret. They seemed to portend far-reaching consequences for his future. Sometimes he tried vaguely to articulate his thoughts to his father, who in turn could only wonder what role destiny would assign to his boy. "Maybe," he said once, "God is planting ideas in your mind which will later motivate you into some great crusade to bless mankind. Who knows?"

In any case Albert found it increasingly difficult to put up with intolerance and meanness in people. He even took the part of an old or weaker cow when stronger members of the herd tried to domineer. He thought of David in the Bible herding sheep and how he later became king, and he wondered if there could be any comparison between his own and David's experience. Could God be getting him ready for something big and important—perhaps to devote his life and energies to some great cause? Whatever it would be, he wanted to be ready; and so he prayed, "Lord, use me as you see fit."

Soon Albert found himself running into prejudice, hate, and narrowmindedness in his own homeland. Here the government did not oppress the people; the people did it to each other. Individuals maddened by religious zeal or bigotry acted cruel and unloving even to the members of their own families.

In one case Albert heard of an irate Catholic family that had poisoned the one and only cow belonging to their daughter because she had married a Lutheran and had threatened to kill the couple's two-year-old son.

In another family an eighteen-year-old daughter had embraced the doctrine of the seventh-day Sabbath. Her father, a dyed-in-the-wool Lutheran, drove her out of the home in midwinter. He even refused her permission to pack any extra clothing. In intense anger he yanked her by the hair from her chair at the breakfast table and thrust her out into the cold, telling her never to come back.

"How could a professed Christian treat a child of his like

that?" Albert pondered. He had seen people treat a dog like that, but never a child.

Albert found himself echoing a declaration he had read once, made by Abraham Lincoln when he saw slaves being auctioned off as cattle. "If I ever get a chance to hit this thing, I'll hit it, and I'll hit it hard." But again he puzzled over how and when he would ever get his chance to do anything about people's meanness to one another and their narrowmindedness in respect to different religious beliefs.

Young Albert felt that a long step toward eliminating intolerant attitudes and toward amicable mutual understanding among people would be taken if people would only talk to each other. One Thursday his father was under the impression that it was Friday. The family, who had become Sabbath keepers, had formed the habit of breaking off work early Friday evening and getting ready for Sabbath. That morning Dad Leiske said, "Boys, hurry and get out into the field. This is Friday, and we have to get a lot of work done before it's time to go home to get ready for the Sabbath." So Albert, along with the other boys, geared for the day off the next day. Mother followed suit by getting the customary rolls and hot milk ready for their "Friday evening" supper.

Next day, however, when the family drove up to the church in Bowdon they found no one else there. Moreover, they found the preacher up on his house shingling his roof! Albert listened as his shocked father argued with the minister over the day of the week. Dad lost the argument and nearly his religion also over the matter.

But his dad needn't have been humiliated, Albert points out, or to have lost a day in the fields. He could have saved himself all this trouble and loss if he had only dialogued with the rest of the family and had been willing to listen to what they had to say. But he always had to have the final word, and nobody dared ask him any questions.

Albert early sensed that he had inherited a liberal portion of his dad's bulldog tenacity and stubborn nature. He found

20

out as he came up against difficult challenges and formidable odds that this trait—if kept in balance—could be an asset. But he had to keep reminding himself whenever he recognized it asserting itself too strongly that inflexibility often needs to be tempered with leniency and with a generous dose of respect for the other person's viewpoint.

Later in life he learned that a greater force than mere logic or common sense had shaped his thinking in this respect. He came to understand how God had led all the way, developing his concepts and charting his destiny. But even at this point, during his growing-up years, some things his mother kept saying and doing gave him an inkling that a divine power figured large in human affairs, especially where people permitted it to happen. And in a simple commitment to his mother's God he promised to try to keep his mind open to that divine influence.

Felt the Hurt

Albert noticed that his mother also possessed strength, though hidden, and she had ways of asserting it when the need arose, even with Dad Leiske.

Albert saw this assertiveness show up during threshing season one year. His dad owned a steam rig and contracted with the owners of neighboring farms to do their threshing—a work that Dad Leiske dearly loved. Albert went along whenever he could, riding with his dad in the big steam engine, with the separator trailing along behind. His dad let him blow the whistle sometimes too, and that really excited the boy. His mother, observing their enjoyment and antics at such times, said they got so involved with what they were doing that they both went crazy and forgot everything else, including shutting gates behind them.

One summer during threshing season Dad Leiske several times left the gate open after driving through, letting the cows into the oat fields. Mother Leiske then had to chase them back into their pasture. Finally she decided she had had enough of such carelessness and laid her strategy to stop it.

She waited until suppertime one evening, when Dad sat down to eat. When she had him where he couldn't get away easily, she let go with both barrels. Albert sat amazed at her sudden nerve.

"You are losing your mind," Albert heard her say. "You

just have no brains anymore when threshing time comes, and you are just absolutely useless around here. You leave the gates open, and the cattle get out. I am about to lose all my religion just following you around and picking up after you."

Albert couldn't believe his ears! He felt like cheering, yet he didn't like to see his father lose his grip on himself either. "I passed John Seibel's place," Dad replied, "and Seibel said, 'I bought a new threshing machine.' When I asked him how it was working, he answered, 'If everything worked as well as the whistle, I would have a good machine.'" Albert could see his father smiling, evidently feeling that by comparing his wife to a working machine whose "whistle" should remain silent except in cases of emergency, he had put her in her place.

But Albert saw in what happened a new and welcome force coming into play. His mother had dared to speak her mind to one whose opinions usually brooked no back talk, and he surely admired her for it. She had struck a blow against intolerance. It left him with a deepening respect for his mother, who became an increasingly greater influence in his life.

Albert recalls how being the "kid brother" in a family of nine children made him feel inferior much of the time. Even the seating arrangement at the family table discriminated against him. "There I sat," he recollects, "at the foot of the table, directly opposite Father and Mother at the far end." Along the sides, four places to each side, sat his brothers and sisters according to age down the line. "I felt a long way from Father," he says thinking back.

"The German background of our family traditionally gave a lot of authority to the older boys," Albert calls to mind. That preordained pecking order contributed to his inferiority complex. Being the youngest boy, he had no defense against this system. Neither his size nor his age came to his rescue. He hardly had any place at all on the totem pole. He

23

felt like an oddity, almost an outcast, and his older brothers rubbed it in.

Under these circumstances Albert found some much needed comfort and support in his mother. This fact he sees as partly explaining why he felt like applauding her that night at the supper table. He saw his practically nonexistent power base becoming somewhat established, with her as an ally. "Politics, maybe you would call it," Albert reflects. "You competed for prestige. You worked toward certain goals and to get a credit rating for yourself." And success, in Albert's estimation, depended on how well you knew the hierarchical structure and on whether you joined up with Mother or Father.

"I went the way of Mother," he concludes. "Mother had a tremendous influence in our family and especially in my life. It may have been that right there in that dining room the germ idea about a town hall meeting got planted in my mind."

At least when Albert grew to manhood and his contacts with the big world outside increased, he saw the family dining room as a microcosm of society at large. There they sat, each busy with his own thoughts and sometimes resentments, but no one talking very much. Afraid to. Afraid of being slapped down. Afraid of being misunderstood or misinterpreted. Afraid of being laughed at. Afraid of incurring Father's displeasure.

Albert had begun to cry out then for someone to break such stalemates and get people talking and listening with respect and cordiality to each other. As he looks back on that early scene in his home, he realizes the need in such situations of a moderator. And to some extent he saw in his mother the potential for such a role. On some occasions she demonstrated the courage and tact and leadership that such a role demands.

"Thank You, dear Lord, for the children," she would pray when it came her turn to say grace at mealtime. "Help them to love You and to do Your will. And keep them from harm and evil this day." Such concern and understanding pulled Albert more and more into the orbit of his mother's influence.

A critical three-year period when Albert suffered from inflammatory rheumatism worried Albert's father a great deal. "How will he ever make it as a farmer?" he fretted. But Albert's mother, typically coming to his rescue, saw in her son's affliction a possible blessing in disguise. "God may have a different plan for this boy," she told her husband.

To Albert she said, "If you don't have the physical stamina to be a farmer, you should plan on getting an education, a Christian education. And then you could go on and become a worker for God—a teacher or a preacher, whatever God leads you to decide on." At ten years of age Albert saw any such future as his mother envisioned to be a long way off.

Through sleepless nights and pain-filled days he despaired of any future at all. During a period of three full years until the age of thirteen he seldom slept in a bed, choosing rather to spend his nights as well as days in a rocking chair to ease the pain. He could hardly move, and his mother sat up with him night after night and took care of his every need. "And she prayed a lot too," Albert remembers.

One winter night, when the temperature outside had dipped to forty below zero, Albert's illness reached a crisis. It seemed to him and his anxious mother that unless they could get medical help he could not last until morning. But the nearest doctor lived in Bowdon, twelve miles away. They sent word to see if he would come.

"We can't possibly get our boy in to you," he heard his mother say, "but could you make it out here to us?" The doctor came out to the Leiske farm in the middle of the night, plowing through deep snow with horses and sleigh.

The doctor did what he could to ease the pain. The

medicine brought enough relief so that Albert fell asleep. But when he awoke, morning had not yet come. Mother, who also had slept little, heard him stir and tiptoed into the living room to spend with her son what she feared might be the last few hours of his life.

But she had by no means given up hope, still believing in God and the power of prayer. Albert vividly remembers what took place next. "She leaned over me," Albert recalls, "and asked me if I would dedicate my life to Christ and His work, if I lived." Then she offered a special prayer dedicating Albert to the Lord, expressing resignation to the possibility that he might not live till morning. In that case she wanted her son to be fully dedicated and ready to go. But she prayed with equal fervor that if he lived he would become a special worker for God and a living testimony of God's miracle-working power the rest of his life.

Albert marks his conversion to God from that rocking-chair experience that night: "From that time on I definitely felt the call of God."

Death, however, did manage to strike the Leiske family during those early years and claim one of his brothers—a tragedy that further motivated Albert to remain true to his mother's God and to his own dedicatory vow.

Leo, about eight years older than Albert and newly married, had started farming on his own not far from where Albert went to school.

A band concert had been scheduled one evening in the schoolhouse, and all the surrounding community had been invited to come. Leo and his young bride came, as did Albert's parents and their children still living at home. Albert, home on break during his first year at the boarding academy in North Dakota, also attended.

During the intermission, Leo and a friend of his stepped outside to a darkened shed in search of a drink of water. In those days schools provided water in ceramic jugs on wooden stands in a room attached to the schoolhouse or located nearby. Community organizers of such events also kept kerosene and gasoline in such jugs for fuel.

Leo's friend, in an attempt to determine which of the jugs contained the drinking water, lighted a match. A violent explosion ripped the little shed, rocked the schoolhouse, and brought the evening's program to a halt. Everybody rushed outside. They found Leo severely injured. His young wife fainted.

Doctors did all they could to save Leo's life. But he had suffered third-degree burns over nearly his entire body. Albert's mother again demonstrated calmness and trust in God's miracle-working power and kept the family's hope alive that again God might intervene. But three days later Leo died.

"I was terribly shaken," Albert recounts. "I renewed my vow to serve God." From that tragic event he also learned to pray more intelligently, having observed that God doesn't always answer the prayers even of righteous people in just the way the petitioners desire.

Albert learned also from the boyhood tragedies in his family how to direct other people's thinking—even that of Christians—when disaster or sorrow strikes, so that they would not lose faith in God. Basically, he learned that everyone in the world will, because of sin and Satan, have his share of trouble. Even Job, called by God a perfect man, did. And John the Baptist suffered cruel martyrdom, even with Jesus geographically nearby. Suffering or even death, he learned, need not be the last chapter in anybody's story. God has promised the righteous something infinitely better than this world. Dwelling in enemy-occupied territory as they do, men on earth will often endure suffering and loss. God permits it, but doesn't cause it. And for sufferers who ask, He provides resources beyond their own to endure, mercifully overruling the enemy's designs.

Albert preached many funeral sermons during his lifetime of ministry, every situation different. But always he

27

drew upon these basic concepts about death and upon God's promises for life hereafter to comfort the mourners—concepts he began to learn in his youth in North Dakota.

About ten years after he began his public evangelism, he held meetings in Livonia, Missouri. On Saturday nights after the service the stores remained open for a while, enabling farmers to do some shopping after the meeting. During this time Albert took advantage of the opportunity to call on the shopkeepers and to visit with people on the street. Always outgoing and sociable, he made many new friends this way.

His rounds always took him past the saloon, and he never failed to stop there too. The proprietor in this case happened to be a lady. She would ask about the meetings, and Albert in turn would wish her God's blessing. Then early one Sunday morning Albert got the sad news that this lady saloonkeeper had shot herself. Friends of hers brought a note which she had left requesting Albert to preach her funeral service.

Characteristically Albert fell back upon the experiences of his boyhood and youth in handling this tragic situation, directing the mourners to God's promises to comfort and sustain all who put their trust in Him, regardless of the circumstances of death. Albert arranged with the funeral director to have the service in the tabernacle. In his sermon he pointed his audience forward to the time when in God's plan death and sorrow would be no more. Touching gently on the question he realized many would be wondering about, he assured his listeners that God in love will deal justly with all people, whether saints or sinners, and left it at that.

In another unique encounter with death, Albert had a colleague and close friend die in his arms. This tragic event took place in Omaha, Nebraska. The two men, attending a church board meeting there, happened to be sitting next to each other. One moment, Albert recalls, they were listening to the chairman, both alert and alive, and the next his friend collapsed and fell over against him, dead. "While it unnerved me for many days," Albert confesses, "it gave me a deeper conviction of the need of living closer to God."

In his own family, thirteen years after his marriage, Albert and his wife lost a baby girl born on the sixth birthday of their only son. Albert understandably reflects upon this loss as something very personal and poignant. It shouldn't have happened, Albert believes, and probably wouldn't have happened today, with the practice of medicine so much more advanced. "She lived just a few hours," Albert recalls. "The problem was toxemia during pregnancy, and they didn't know how to handle it then. Our six-year-old son cried bitterly. It was very sad."

Bishop Leiske knew as the years rolled on that someday either he or Mae would likely be left to walk the rest of the way alone. Involvement as a minister in the losses and sorrows of others had taught him that death respects no one, saint or sinner, young or old. But when after fifty-four years together, he lost his Mae, his bereavement seemed more crushing than he could bear.

"The bottom just dropped out of my life." The sudden-ness of Mae's death made it harder for him to handle. On Wednesday evening just before her surgery the next day, he visited her in the hospital. There he committed his dear one into the care of the Great Physician as they prayed together and kissed her good night, fully expecting her back home in a few days following a normal recovery.

Instead came that telephone call. Dead. He would never hear her cheery voice again, never go riding with her in their specially made "bicycle for two," never hand her his Bible as he walked down the aisle to shake hands at the door following a sermon, never feel the encouragement of her smile, or never be able to turn to her for advice.

Who would take care of his bookkeeping now? Who would oversee his domestic affairs? Who would handle the many things that were the domain of "Mother Superior," the First Lady of the Town Hall organization, this queen in his life?

Albert hardly dared to believe what seemed to be happening a year or so later when a replica of his Mae showed up at a party he had been invited to attend. He had been praying for someone to fill the void he felt so poignantly. "Let her be the widow of an evangelist, Lord," he had petitioned. It seemed to him that only a person with this qualification could fill the bill—someone who could understand his past and share his hopes for the future.

He felt his heart skip a beat when he learned that this gracious lady at the party had indeed been a minister's wife, her husband dead some fifteen years. Moreover, she had worked as an administrative secretary and knew bookkeeping. He had never seen her before, or she him; but something told them both that their coming together at that party had been providential. In a matter of a few months Wana Schneider became the answer to Albert's prayer. "And now," says Albert, "we are moving ahead together."

Albert, after years of experience, freely concedes that no one can live as long as he has without a lot of trouble along the way. You have to expect it, he philosophizes. Even the Bible says that if a man by reason of strength lives fourscore years, he will experience "labour and sorrow." Psalm 90:10. "During the last ten especially," he adds.

Despite the trouble spots in his eventful life, the aches and disappointments, he refuses to dwell on them. "Why waste time talking or thinking about them?" he asks. To him there are so many more pleasant and beautiful things to talk about—happy memories to reflect on. Whenever anybody asks him how he feels or how things are going, he answers radiantly, "Fine! Great! Top of the world!"

He rejoices in the goodness of God, to whose service he dedicated his life while propped up in a rocking chair, some seventy years ago.

Counted the Pennies

"Make mine cornflakes and cream," said Evangelist Albert Leiske when it came his turn to give his order to the waitress. He had gone with a group of his fellow workers for dinner at a popular eating place one evening after an evangelistic meeting. He gave his order almost without thinking, as this dietary peculiarity had practically become a habit. But the startled waitress thought she had heard wrong. That item didn't even appear on the menu, and it sounded so strangely different from what the others in the group had ordered.

But that's what Albert had said, and that's what he wanted. And—after some insistence—that's what he got.

That's what Albert had ordered years before when a boy growing up on his father's farm in North Dakota. Father Gottlieb Leiske had established the custom of providing recreation for his growing family of nine children by taking them to town at certain lull times during the year. Albert looked forward to these special reward trips following periods of hard work on the farm.

Albert remembers the routine well. Before leaving for town, his dad would give each child some money to spend, to spend for whatever he wanted.

"Now here's your money," he would say as he pulled out his old snap-button pocketbook bulging with coins. "Come get it, and make sure you don't lose it."

Albert would take his place next to last in the line to wait his turn. His dad, then, following the old German traditon of showing preference to the firstborn, started with Jacob, his eldest, and then stairstepped down the line in order of age—Lizzie, Aldridge, Leo, and so on.

The amount too differed according to age, Albert recalls. Jacob and Lizzie each received a quarter, Aldridge and Leo twenty cents, and George and William fifteen cents. Albert would hold out his cupped hands for Dad and then would carefully tuck the money away into the deepest pocket he had and cover it with a handkerchief or something so it wouldn't shake out and get lost on the way to town.

"To us three littlest kids Dad gave only a dime each," Albert vividly remembers. In fact, he painfully remembers it, because the differentiation in amount added to the hurt he felt in being discriminated against as the "kid brother." Sometimes Albert got his money in pennies instead of a ten-cent piece. He didn't mind that, because it seemed like a larger amount. He knew his money well enough, though, to know that it only *seemed* larger. He still would have to count his pennies, for in reality he had only that one small thin dime as far as value was concerned, and he would have to stretch it as far as he could.

Albert's brothers and sisters always headed straight for the candy counter in the grocery store where their parents traded. Albert too found himself tempted by the colorful assortment of goodies—licorice sticks, chocolate bars, gum-drops of different colors, red-and-white-striped candy canes, plus Cracker Jacks with a tempting prize in each box. It was enough to make any child's eyes bulge and mouth water.

But Albert bought cornflakes instead. "You could buy a box of cornflakes for ten cents in those days," he says. "I would buy cornflakes instead of candy because it would last longer. And then at home I would take advantage of the free cream and milk."

Then during the weeks that his box lasted, Albert would

have a bowl of cornflakes every now and then with cream and milk on it, and his brothers and sisters could only watch him eat it. Albert's mother encouraged this kind of thriftiness in her youngest son and saw to it that none of the other children filched any of his cornflakes.

On the farm where Albert grew up the family had enough food, but plain and monotonously the same throughout most of the year. Except for the addition of fresh vegetables for a short period during summer and early fall, the dinner diet consisted mainly of bread, meat, potatoes, and sauerkraut. For breakfast they had oatmeal or grits. They also had gravy. Everybody had gravy in those days, as Albert remembers his childhood, at least around where he lived. Gravy on bread, gravy on mashed potatoes, and (a staple in many homes) gravy on hot soda biscuits for breakfast.

"Do you see why I treasured my cornflakes and made them last as long as I could?" Albert asks. "I really had to make those pennies stretch."

"And do you see," he adds with a twinkle in his eye, "why I still like to order a bowl of cornflakes and cream sometimes, even when it's not on the menu?"

Little Albert felt the pinch of poverty when it came to clothing also. The whole family did for that matter, but especially Albert, because of his having been born between two girls. Reflecting on his childhood, Albert remembers how he rejoiced when he finally became "a boy"—that is, when he finally received his first pair of pants.

Always before that, he had to wear dresses, hand-me-downs from next-older Theresa. Clothes always had to be handed down from one child to the next as long as they had any wear left in them. Albert barely escaped the mortification of having to wear his sister's dresses to school when he turned six.

Not long after being promoted to full boyhood, Albert began to do his full share of chores on his father's farm. He had to get up at four in the morning, along with the rest of the menfolk, to help with the milking and feeding and cleaning barns. He remembers milking at least five or six cows out of a total of twenty or so as his share.

Once, when he hurt his hand his brothers let him off. "You couldn't milk by hand, as of course everyone did in those days," Albert points out, "if you had something wrong with your hands." This temporary good fortune gave him the idea of feigning a hurt hand every now and then. But his older brothers soon caught on. "If they decided that my hands were not really sore, they made me milk," Albert remembers, "and that was that." The older Leiske boys had a lot of authority, especially in the cow barn.

All of Albert's brothers and sisters, except the baby sister, had to hustle from early to late to accomplish everything that had to be done on the farm. Albert's father, though not a taskmaster, ran a precision-timed program, with no one excused except for sickness. "God helps those who help themselves," he said.

Albert came into the sod-house home of Gottlieb and Elisabeth Leiske about sixteen years after they immigrated from Russia and settled in North Dakota. He remembers hearing his parents tell of their first years on the homestead. Accustomed to hard work in the old country, they tackled the challenges of their new life with vigor and enthusiasm.

First, they had to build their home, using materials readily available. Albert remembers well the shape and features of the one his parents built, for it remained standing on the farm several years after a new frame building had taken its place. The pioneers simply plowed and cut the sod into pieces twelve to eighteen inches wide, two or three feet long, and four to six inches thick. They then stacked these pieces one upon another to make the walls, the same way a bricklayer lays brick. They slanted the end walls to a point at the top to provide a pitch for the roof, the peaked points at the two ends of the house being connected by a ridgepole to support the roof.

"The ridgepole cost us almost as much as the rest of the house put together," Dad Leiske told Albert. "It had to be shipped in, and we had to pay cash for it. The rest of the materials we got right from the prairie."

Albert never tired of hearing his dad tell about the great blizzard of 1888, less than three years after his parents had settled on the homestead, and only a year or so after his oldest brother, Jacob, had been born. One of their neighbors nearly lost his life that terrible night. Seeing the storm coming up, he had decided to take a shortcut home across the Leiske fields. But the storm overtook him. The swirling snow completely blinded him, and he lost all sense of direction. The mounting drifts made it hard to keep going.

Albert could hardly bear the suspense at this point, though he had heard the story many times and knew exactly how it would end. The man, almost exhausted and ready to give up, suddenly ran smack into the Leiske house. Not knowing for sure whether he had bumped into a house or a barn or just a stone fence, he started feeling his way along with his hands, until he felt a recessed area in the wall. He reached out in several directions, hoping to find a latch or a string. And then he fell with a thud, banging his head against the door, where inside the Leiskes sat around the fire trying to keep warm.

"What if you had not heard that bang above the howling of the storm?" Albert would ask. "Or what if you had decided not to open the door? Or what if—?"

Albert could think of many possible outcomes. But he always breathed a sigh of relief when Dad ended up by telling the real outcome—how they brought the frozen man inside, revived him, and saved his life.

"Whew! that was too close," Albert would say. And the thoughts of what his father would have stumbled over the next morning gave him the creeps.

Such accounts of near disaster left a fearful impression on Albert's young mind. Sometimes he would awaken from a nightmare in which he would be the victim about to be overtaken by one of the tragedies he had heard the older people talk about.

Many menaces threatened them and their livelihood, making life an ongoing contest against the elements. Albert heard words such as *cloudbursts, tornadoes,* and *prairie fires,* and he wondered when one of these calamities might come upon them.

Where would they turn for food, he pondered, if a hailstorm should flatten their fields just before harvest? This tragedy had actually happened, he heard, depriving hundreds of farmers of their only source of cash income for a whole year.

Except around harvest time the thoughts of drought made every cloud a welcome sight to Albert. That story in the Bible about Elijah praying for rain (1 Kings 18) meant something special to him. Every ten years or so, Albert had heard the old-timers say, you could expect a severe drought. This possibility worried Albert a great deal.

Once already in his young life he had experienced a short drought one summer, and he could imagine what a sustained one would be like. No hay in the barns for the cattle, just emptiness. He had heard the wind whistle through the cracks of their barn in late spring when most of the hay had been used up.

"It made an 'o-o-o-o-o-o' sound," he recollected, "an eerie, haunting sound, that gave you a sense of forlornness in the pit of your stomach." He knew that Dad and everybody else would have to count the pennies if the country would ever be hit by a severe drought.

One particular summer Albert frequently came upon his parents hovering over a batch of papers kept in a drawer of the kitchen cabinet, their faces creased with anxiety, their voices muted. Albert picked up a sentence now and then that confirmed his suspicion that the problem had something to do with money. "What have we gone and done now?" "More than we can chew." "We shouldn't have let the man talk us into it." Prayers at family worship reflected this concern also. "Please, dear Lord, send us rain," he heard often during a long dry spell. Prayers were answered and rain came.

But then as the grain ripened for harvest, with only days to go before it would be ready to cut, nobody wanted rain, for rain at this time would ruin the wheat. One evening when dark clouds began to roll up in the west, Albert's father petitioned "the Lord of the harvest" to keep disaster away just a few days longer. "Don't let it rain or hail," he earnestly implored. "Please, not now!"

Albert finally figured out the primary cause of his parents' stress. His father had bought a gasoline-powered tractor that spring to get the plowing done faster. But the machine had something wrong with it; half of the time it wouldn't start. Father couldn't afford wasting time getting it fixed. In addition, the man at the equipment store had talked them into investing in a big steam engine, assuring them it could pull anything they hitched it to. It would pull five plows easily, the man had said, and to Albert's father that seemed the solution for getting their 2000 acres of wheatland plowed in time for sowing.

So Albert's parents had gone ahead and signed the papers. But when they went into the field with the big machine the next day it nearly sank into oblivion. There had been a lot of rain that spring, and this huge steam engine simply bogged down in the damp earth, and there it stayed.

Dad Leiske's nerves became taut as rubber bands. He had mortgaged a large share of the anticipated wheat crop for these two machines, and neither of them worked. Albert saw beads of perspiration on his father's forehead and sensed his deep frustration.

In desperation Albert's parents talked to the man at the store again. Then they called the whole family into a counseling session. Albert couldn't understand the total implications of it all, but he joined with the others in agreeing to take the man's advice and buy still another gasoline tractor, this one equipped with extra wide wheels and guaranteed not to sink.

Dad Leiske then made the final investment, even going so far out on a limb this time as to mortgage the farm. Even as a small boy Albert picked up these tensions and realized that somehow the family would be in deep trouble if they failed to harvest a good crop that year. "We were entirely dependent on God," he reflected later with a mature understanding of the odds the family had been up against during that crisis.

"But it all came out all right in the end," Albert recalls with still a feeling of relief as he tells the story. "We harvested a bumper crop and paid off all the notes at one shot. Father managed to save the farm and his own operation and everything." And at family worship that fall Albert remembers hearing special prayers of gratitude for it all. "We balanced for a few weeks on the edge of a steep precipice, but God in mercy pulled us back from disaster."

Another experience of financial stress, Albert recalls, stemmed from the organization in Bowdon of a farmers' union store. Ever feeling the need of saving a penny wherever they could, Albert's parents fell for the line that a cooperative owned and operated by the farmers themselves could provide groceries and other necessities at far cheaper rates, cutting out the middleman's profit. It cost each family two hundred dollars to join, but the promoters had assured the Leiskes and others that they would get their money back in no time from the huge savings they would realize from the lower prices.

"We pictured our store," Albert says in a reflective mood, "as something like our cupboard at home. We thought we could go behind the counter and get what we wanted, because it belonged to us."

But the whole thing turned out to be a complete flop. The other stores met the threatened competition by lowering their prices to sacrifice levels for a while just when the farmers' store opened up for business. The farmers, including the Leiskes, not realizing the intricacies of competitive marketing and wanting to save every penny they could, bought their stuff where they could get it the cheapest.

So the farmers' store went broke. And the Leiske family lost their two hundred dollars—a lot of money in those days.

As Albert grew older, he still had to keep on counting the pennies. Never did there seem to be enough money to go around, and always clothes seemed to be the one thing the family felt they could sacrifice on.

Albert remembers the evening event at the town square in Heaton during his last year in grade school. Awkward and thin at that age, he never looked dressed up anyway, even with his best clothes on. He had been invited that night by the town fathers to give a patriotic speech at this special gathering.

"I accepted," he says, "but in those days we were so poor that I had only one collar, and that happened to be in the dirty clothes basket at the time waiting to be washed." What a dither to be in, Albert recalls, but his mother came to the rescue.

"Wear Dad's collar," she said. Dad Leiske, a big man, wore a size sixteen and a half, Albert a fourteen. But Albert wore his dad's collar that night, with his skinny neck sticking out through it making him look like a scarecrow. The lecture went over big anyway, he remembers; the town banker pronounced him an upcoming orator.

Because of Albert's upbringing amidst surroundings of poverty and social inequalities, it became natural for him to reflect a strong identification with the underdog. The intensity of this identification motivated him throughout his ministry to do whatever he could toward social betterment. He learned also to find within himself unexpected and untapped resources upon which to draw in times of peril and privation.

But above it all, as Albert sums it up, those difficult years on the prairies of North Dakota led him to trust in God. "We looked upon our poverty-stricken days," he says, "as a lesson from God. We learned to place our confidence upon the Lord."

Albert sees the events of his boyhood and youth as the pieces God providentially put together to make his life a beautiful mosaic of service. And if some of these pieces in God's sight had to be the rigors of poverty and hard work, Albert says that's fine with him and rejoices in the wisdom and goodness of God. "We have a wonderful God," Albert reaffirms. "From His great and calm eternity He ordered for me that which in His providence He knew to be best."

Made a Total Commitment

Albert learned a text from the Bible with a question in it during his early days of austerity on the prairies of North Dakota: "Can God furnish a table in the wilderness?" Psalm 78:19. He found the answer to be Yes. Not only at that time but again and again since. He drew upon that text repeatedly during his ministry in giving people assurance of God's providential care in times of stress—financial or otherwise. It became one of his favorites.

"Of course God can set a table in the wilderness," Albert firmly asserts, particularly when people get into the wilderness as a consequence of walking under the direction of God. Albert does not encourage the presumptuous hope that God will set a table for the person who walks contrary to God's will into the wilderness. Neither does he encourage any slothful expectation that God will do for a man what the man can and should do for himself in setting his own table.

Albert early in life developed a contempt for lazy people, an absolute distaste for a laggardly, leisurely pace in his associates. He grew up in an environment where man competed against nature for survival. If a farmer failed to get his plowing done and seed sown at the opportune time in spring, he had to take the consequences of a poor harvest in the fall. And nobody felt too sorry for him. People simply said he got what he deserved and left him to his fate.

Albert's familiarity with the Bible and his application of its principles to daily life began in early childhood. He can't recall a time when the old leather-bound copy that his parents brought with them from Russia did not occupy an honored place on the parlor table.

When he was about the age of eight, Albert remembers that his parents began studying that old family Bible more intently. An itinerant preacher with a long beard had held religious meetings in the community schoolhouse and taught the people that the second coming of Jesus could take place in their lifetime. He had also taught them that the Bible required Christians to keep the seventh day of the week as the Sabbath. During that time Albert often saw his parents with the Bible open before them, turning to the texts the preacher had read. Sometimes at night when it came time for Albert to go to bed, they would be studying, poring over the Scriptures by the light of their kerosene lamp. They wanted to make sure that the texts read the same in their German Bible and that the preacher hadn't left out anything.

From then on, Albert's father and mother began having family worship in the home and going to church on Saturday. The Bible became the center of their new religious beliefs and the book from which they instructed their children.

"We had regular worship every morning for about ten to fifteen minutes," Albert recollects. "First, Father read the Scriptures, and then we prayed the Lord's Prayer together, the whole family kneeling in a circle as Father led out."

On Friday nights at the beginning of the Sabbath, the family spent a whole hour in devotion, including the singing of favorite hymns. Albert remembers the harmony, each child carrying a part with a natural, inborn ability.

"These worship periods greatly inspired me to be a minister," Albert says, thinking back. But he wondered how he would ever grow one of those long beards.

Hearing his name in prayer during family worship made a deep impression on Albert. Once he even heard it in his mother's prayer apart from those family gatherings. He passed her window one evening and heard her voice in prayer. "She was all alone in there," he says, "praying especially for me."

Albert didn't attend a church school during his elementary grades. Nor does he remember learning memory verses in his childhood. But his parents so stimulated his interest in the Bible from the time he first went to school and learned to read that by the age of nine he already knew the names of all the books of the Old and New Testaments in order and understood the basic use of marginal references.

His older brother George, for some reason hadn't done quite so well. Albert happened along one evening and found George in trouble trying to get a talk ready for a meeting of the Young People's Society. He helped him to locate the texts he wanted to use, also assisting him in finding related ones he didn't even know about by using the marginal references.

Albert doesn't recall at what age he owned his first Bible. He thinks that probably his parents gave him one during his three-year illness. At that time of forced leisure, especially when recovery began after his mother's prayer, he read everything he could get his hands on. He treasured God's promises to heal and restore and rejoiced that these had been fulfilled for him. He underlined special ones, such as "With God all things are possible." Mark 10:27. He learned scores of these texts together with their references by heart.

His encyclopedic knowledge of the Bible based on his almost photographic memory, for which Albert years later became noted as an evangelist, must have had its beginning in those preteen and teen years. One of his ministerial associates recalls that he can remember only once when Albert Leiske couldn't locate the text he needed on the spur of the moment. Also Albert's lifelong habit of spending a specified period each day in prayer and Bible study must have begun then.

Albert's reading at that time also included a great deal of history. He developed a particular fondness for Abraham Lincoln, whose championship of the oppressed helped to motivate him to set a similar life goal.

Albert attended elementary school in the same schoolhouse where the Adventist preacher had held his meetings—a typical one-room school, with one teacher for all eight grades. Some mornings the teacher assigned him the job of putting the flag up. It meant something special to him to do this and to stand at attention with the other twenty or so pupils and repeat the pledge of allegiance.

"With liberty and justice for all," they concluded in unison. The words to the other kids probably meant little beyond the ritual of the moment. But for Albert they reverberated with challenge, challenge which would eventually set his feet marching to the beat of a drummer different from that of most of his fellow students.

Albert seems from his earliest boyhood days to have cherished a deep concern for American freedoms and democracy. Responding to heart promptings, he once temporarily converted the hayloft in his father's barn into a "meeting place." He surrounded the platform and the speaker's stand with an array of American flags. Above the speaker's stand in foot-high letters he displayed the slogan "For Freedom and Democracy."

Six years later, when graduating from Sheyenne River Academy, at Harvey, North Dakota, Albert came on stage again marching to this unusual drumbeat. On behalf of his fellow graduates, he presented the class gift to the school.

"We have departed from the usual custom," he said in his little speech, "and have prepared a service flag." The flag had twelve stars, each star representing a student who had gone from the academy responding to his country's call. The class, under Albert's leadership, had thus underwritten the ideals of freedom and democracy, honoring those who had given their lives to perpetuate these rights.

In September 1917 Albert had said Good-bye to his family and journeyed forty-two miles to Harvey to enroll as an academy freshman. The real distance, however, in this case had to be calculated in terms other than miles. Albert found himself entering a different world. He would now be learning "to become someone in life"—a philosophy that had tinted the horizons of his thinking since childhood. More particularly, he would be training to become "someone" for God, following through on that promise he had made that winter night in the rocking chair as he and his mother prayed.

But Albert soon found that merely making the journey didn't make him a different person. He still had a long way to go to fulfill on that promise, with many a battle with self to fight.

"I had all the devilishness that the devil ever put into a man," he said later in thinking back on those days. "Not wicked from the standpoint of real wickedness, but up to more tricks in five minutes than the average fellow could think of in twenty-four hours."

Furthermore, although Albert had heard the drumbeat of the Divine, he hadn't yet made up his mind fully to march to it. "I was normal," he says in retrospect, "and had a tremendous struggle dedicating my life fully to God." He had to come to that place where he would be willing to stand for principle even if he had to stand alone.

Evidently Albert lived up to his own estimation of himself when it came to playing tricks. His classmates, and unfortunately also the faculty, soon regarded him as a ringleader among the boys in mischief making and frivolity. "He was noted for his pranks and gab," one of his schoolfellows later said about him.

One Friday night Albert decided to crawl through a transom into the kitchen, where he thought he could get some cinnamon rolls. A bunch of the boys had challenged him, and all of course planned to enjoy the feast together. As he struggled to worm his way through the narrow window, his feet kicking away in mid-air, the principal came along. Of course, his "friends" all scampered and left him to face the music alone.

"Where are you going, Albert?" the principal demanded, grabbing the flouncing legs.

Characteristically quick on the trigger, Albert shot back from the other side othe transom, "I'm going back!" The incident understandably left doubts in the principal's mind about Albert's intentions and trustworthiness.

On another occasion Albert led out in a rather mean conspiracy to make a naive young fellow the butt of a rude joke. This fellow, named Stern, wanted a girl friend, a privilege severely restricted by the school rules. But the boys, including Albert, got around the rules prohibiting communication between couples by writing notes to their girl friends and having them delivered by an ally.

So Albert told Stern to pick himself out a girl friend and write her a note, and he would get it to her. Stern chose Mabel and wrote to her. But instead of delivering as promised, Albert brought the note to his cronies in the plot, and they all read and laughed over it together. Then they wrote one purporting to be from Mabel and delivered it to Stern, wording it so as to give him heartthrobs.

This went on for some time, the group enjoying a big joke at Stern's expense. Then Albert suggested to Stern that he buy his girl a box of candy, telling him that he had just bought one for his girl. So Stern did, giving it to Albert to deliver. But by this time Albert felt that the joke had gone far enough, and he called Stern to his room along with the conspirators and confessed the whole thing. Everybody had yet another good laugh, even Stern, who took it as a good sport, though Albert could see the hurt through the laughter.

Albert enjoyed his studies at the academy, particularly his Bible classes. He made good grades too, generally placing near the top on the honor roll. He meant business even though he didn't necessarily convince all of the faculty.

He carried a burden on his heart to share what he had learned with others. And so he went canvassing one summer vacation, selling a book called *Bible Readings for the Home Circle*. In the rural territory assigned to him, he went from farmhouse to farmhouse on horseback. He earned a scholarship that summer, but more significant to his developing Christian experience, he learned to trust God more fully—depending upon Him for guidance throughout the day and for a place to stay at night.

This adventure in seeking to bless others resulted in a reflex action on his own soul. This outcome stemmed partly from demonstrating day after day in his canvass a picture feature called "The Game of Life." The picture showed a young man about to make a fatal move, with Satan egging him on but with Christ also hovering near to hold him back. Albert saw himself in that picture and realized that sooner or later he would have to come to grips with himself and make his ultimate decision for or against Christ's way of life.

Albert's turn to make his crucial move came during his junior year. Toward the end of that school year one of the seniors fell ill with pneumonia and died. The faculty decided to close school the day of the funeral, giving the principle and the teachers an opportunity to attend, which meant a drive of nearly a hundred miles to the boy's home church.

The faculty left the students on their honor, instructing them to either study or mourn, but in no case to leave the campus. And they appointed one of the older boys to be in charge and to give a report to the faculty upon their return.

Some of the boys decided to play ball instead of mourn. Albert, who had planned to join them, suddenly got word that his brother Aldridge, on his way to Canada, wanted to see him in Harvey. So Albert left the campus without permission and went into town to see his brother.

When the principal returned, the student in charge dutifully gave his report, but embellished it with a few rumors that showed Albert and the ballplayers in a bad light. The story he told amounted to a distortion of the truth.

So the faculty proceeded to deal with the matter as a serious crime, when actually it amounted to only a misdemeanor. "They could have campus-bound us for a week or so as punishment," Albert observes, "and we would have seen the justice of that." But instead the faculty met and picked out four students whom they considered the ringleaders in the "rebellion" and expelled them. And Albert, already having gained a reputation as a ringleader in most mischief making on campus, got caught in the dragnet.

Albert resented this injustice very much. The four boys, who could not even write their final examinations, thus faced the threat of losing their whole year's work. To Albert the punishment seemed harder than he could bear, and he went away bitter. He especially resented the lies the student in charge had told. In fact, he looked him up before he left and really cleaned up on him.

Albert took the train out to Walla Walla, Washington, determined never to set foot on campus at Harvey again. In his bitterness he even pondered severing connections with his parents' church altogether. "What an intolerant bunch!" he thought. What they had done to him and his buddies flew right in the face of all the principles of democracy and justice he had espoused and orated about. He wanted nothing more to do with such an outfit.

But then he thought of that checkerboard game pictured in the book. He saw himself as the one about to make a fatal move. He thought of his mother and her prayers, especially her prayer dedicating him to the Lord's service that night when he almost died.

He came to himself in a "far country" on the West Coast, and he began to say some things to himself. He remembered one of the texts he had learned in Bible class, one which later became so much a key text in his preaching that he used it in nearly every sermon—Isaiah 55:7, 8.

"Let the wicked forsake his way," it said, "and the unrighteous man his thoughts: and let him return unto the Lord." That's what God wants me to do, he meditated. And then he noted the ensuing promise: "He will have mercy upon him; and . . . he will abundantly pardon."

"What more could a man want?" he thought. If only he could have the assurance of God's forgiveness, it wouldn't matter what the authorities back at the academy thought about him.

Then he read the next verse: "My thoughts are not your thoughts, neither are your ways my ways." God is trying to tell me something, he mused, and I had better listen. He didn't spare my life that night back there on the farm for nothing. He has appointed me a part in His great plan of preaching His gospel of pardon to a lost world, and He wants me to line up with that plan.

The more Albert thought, the more a decision began to firm up in his mind. He saw what his next move in the game of life ought to be. He would go back to Sheyenne River Academy and ask for another chance to make good. He didn't know what the other three "ringleaders" would do, but it didn't matter. He would stand on his own.

"Please, dear Lord," he prayed, "take all this bitterness and wrath out of my heart and give me Thy meekness, Thy forbearance, Thy love. And leave me not alone to misinterpret the motives of the faculty in the way they dealt with me. Give me courage to go back and take the consequences."

"And may they be willing," he added, "to do what the text says You would do if I return to You. Make them willing to abundantly pardon."

So the next fall Albert went back to the academy. He drove there in a Ford car his parents had given him. "When you get there, trade it in for your tuition," they had instructed him. His parents, especially his mother, backed him in his plans all the way, and he felt the strength of their influence.

As he drove onto the campus, he wondered if he would have the courage to go through with the deal. Memories of the spring episode threw up straw men in his imagination: Maybe they'll make me stand barefoot for three days outside their castle door before they'll even talk with me. Or maybe they'll give me the third degree. Or maybe—.

But Albert had made up his mind. He would go to the faculty and say, "I made a fool of myself last year. But I would like to come back and make good. Please give me another chance."

He felt relieved to find the principal alone in his office—and in a kind, receptive mood. He didn't even let Albert go on and complete his speech. Maybe he, too, had had some second thoughts about the severity of the punishment meted out the spring before.

Anyway, Albert got the chance he requested, and he did make good. That year turned out to be a mountain-peak year in his experience. Most of all, he discovered with joy that when God changes a person, He really changes him—makes him an entirely new creation, as he had read in 2 Corinthians 5:17. Finally Albert had gone all the way with Christ to walk in His ways and to be guided by His thoughts. He had put on Christ's yoke and found it easy; he had taken up the cross and found it light.

Near the close of the year Albert responded to an altar call at the end of the school's special week of prayer, committing his life again to the Lord's service. Some ten years had gone by since he had done it that memorable winter night back home.

"This time it's for real and for good," he vowed. "I will never again disgrace my Lord." And shortly thereafter he sealed his commitment by being baptized, the only student to be baptized that year. In making his total commitment he would follow his Lord's example of perfect dependence upon

God's power and complete submission to His will.

Then came graduation and commencement, May 1922, and for Albert commencement really meant commencement, a beginning. He had already reached the age of twenty-one, having lost three precious years during his boyhood illness. Now he felt he had to be off and running to make up for lost time.

"If you operate and move under the providence of God," he said, "God has a purpose for your life." And Albert wanted to get going in fulfilling that purpose. From that day forward his life became a series of goals which, when realized, became part of another far-reaching and exciting goal. Always his central focus was on reaching as many souls as possible with the gospel of God's grace, which had so miraculously transformed his own life.

He felt he ought not to take time for further education, yet people whom he respected advised him to do so. At camp meeting he met Professor J. B. Penner, head of the German department at Clinton Theological Seminary in Missouri, who eventually persuaded him. Albert spent the 1923-24 school year at Clinton. It proved a fruitful year, he reflects, because he acquired such valuable skills as choir directing and choral singing, plus further training and practice in public speaking.

Albert had already spent nine months—the school year prior to that—teaching school, as well as two summers in normal college learning how to teach. So he felt he had finally acquired enough educaton and training and that now he ought to get going on the real thing—evangelism.

But then suddenly he realized, or maybe some of the older brethren helped him to realize, that he didn't have a wife yet. And, further, he read in the Bible that every bishop "must be . . . husband of one wife." 1 Timothy 3:2. (Of course, he hadn't become a bishop—not yet.) Nevertheless, he eagerly responded to a call from his home state, North Dakota, to participate in evangelism that first summer and fall after finishing his year at Clinton. His first assignment was at Devil's Lake.

Here again Albert would see the unfolding of God's providence in a way he had never dreamed could happen. He remembered his favorite text: "My thoughts are not your thoughts, neither are your ways my ways."

So with confidence he walked into the wilderness alone, believing God would provide a companion for him—just the right one—to walk with him, according to His own will and purpose and in His own time.

Found the Right Girl

"That was Albert's way of life, and Mae was right there beside him," recalls Kathryn, who knew Albert in the summer of 1924 in Devil's Lake, North Dakota, and who herself conceivably might have been the one "right there beside" Albert. But the words refer instead to the beautiful relationship that began back then between Albert and Mae and which lasted more than half a century.

Albert must have noticed Kathryn that summer. He had joined the evangelistic team headed by Raymond Bresee at Devil's Lake and so had she. The North Dakota Conference had called Albert to lead the singing and Kathryn to play the piano.

Albert had turned twenty-three that spring. He had completed his training at Clinton Theological Seminary, ready now to launch out into the ministry. Albert, still single, had experienced the normal flooding of the body's hormones and felt the time had come when he ought to get married. But to whom? That question weighed heavily on his mind. Daily he knelt in prayer, seeking God's guidance.

He had dated girls during his school days at Harvey and at Clinton. But to this point he had not found the right one for a life companion.

One girl at the academy had become special to him. In fact, he allowed himself to get rather serious about her—a case of typical teenage infatuation. He would plan his moves to synchronize with hers, so that they would just "happen" to be at the same places about the same time. And his heart would beat a little faster when she smiled at him from across the dining room. Once for Valentine's Day he spent nearly his last money for a box of candy for her, and somehow he sneaked it to her along with an appropriate note. As time went on, he became so enraptured by her that he could be seen gazing off into space when he should have been studying.

But this girl suddenly cooled toward him, almost breaking his heart. He suspected that maybe his rude joke on the Stern boy might have had something to do with her change of attitude. He learned that she chummed with Mabel, the girl Stern had chosen, at Albert's instigation, to be his special "girl friend." He learned also that the two girls had gotten wind of how Albert had tricked Stern into sending Mabel notes and candy, which of course she never got and which she would have indignantly spurned anyway.

Albert evidently let his crushed feelings show on the outside, prompting his friends to try and cheer him up. "Don't let it get you down, Al," they said. "Girls are like streetcars. If you miss one, another will come along in twenty minutes." Albert chuckled mechanically, but his face still wore that funereal look.

Later Albert became friendly with still another girl at the academy. But this time he didn't let himself fall quite so hard. He didn't like getting hurt. But again he found himself planning ways to get together. When it came time to go into the surrounding community to solicit funds for missionary work, for example, he had a part in assigning the various groups to their cars and territories. Of course, he just happened to find himself in the same car as the object of his favor.

Another of his interests was one who lived outside the girls' residence with relatives. Albert particularly enjoyed going to this home on Saturday afternoons to sing. This group singing reminded him of Friday evenings back home on the farm. When he saw this girl enjoying this kind of Christian fellowship too, it gave him a romantic feeling toward her. The fact that they had this interest in common seemed to be telling him something. He liked the way she sang the alto part too. Her German background also seemed a point in her favor as he weighed the pros and cons regarding her suitability as a possible choice.

But Albert's academy days had come and gone without his having found the right girl. "I had girl friends also in college," he remembers. "But I never decided on anybody." He kept on praying, however, that God would direct him in finding just the one who would help him the most in his lifework as a minister of the gospel.

He remembered reading somewhere that Satan tries his best to get couples wholly unsuited to each other united in marriage. And he had seen homes where, in his estimation, the devil had done well, homes where incompatibility and clash of interests seemed to result in discord and constant contention. He didn't want a home like that.

Now in the summer of 1924 Albert landed at Devil's Lake. The coincidence of the name with his present concern struck him as funny, making him smile at his own predicament.

He saw his chances of finding a life companion measuring up to his ideals and requirements growing slim indeed. If he had not found someone in school, where the student body included many girls, what chance would have have out here? He dreaded the thought of spending his life as a celibate. He couldn't see himself in the role of a monk.

Then Kathryn had come along. But Albert soon found that this "clicking" business in boy-and-girl relationships has to be a two-way street. No doubt, the two had much in common. Both belonged to the same religious faith. Both loved music, and both found enjoyment and fulfillment in using their talents for God. Both had grown up in North

Dakota, with similar tastes and backgrounds. And now both had responded to calls to assist in public evangelism.

Albert found it easy to interpret these similarities as indications of God's providence favoring a possible romance. But he noticed that Kathryn expressed no such thoughts whatsoever. From things she would say, he picked up signals quite to the contrary. After her summer with the evangelistic team she planned to go on with her education, that being her chief aspiration at the moment.

Albert kept on praying.

Then the meetings in the tent began, with Al, as he now preferred to be called, doing his full share leading out in the singing at night and visiting people during the day. At one home he called on a Mrs. Sneesby, who chose not to invite him inside. She wanted nothing to do with this new religion. He learned that she and her daughters went to the Methodist church. Her husband, a police officer, had died a few months earlier after being shot during a post-office robbery. Albert also learned from the brief conversation at the door that one daughter, Mae, still lived at home but was away for a few weeks for medical treatment. He remembered also that this widowed mother had mentioned that her absent daughter worked at a bank in Devil's Lake when home.

Two weeks or so later Al remembered his visit to this lady's home when a young woman called at the tent, bringing a young man with her. Her name was Mae. She had met the young man, Al learned, in Rochester, Minnesota, where she had gone for treatment and had found him interested in the Bible. He had stopped at her home for a day, on his way through town, for further discussions on the Bible. Having heard about the tent meetings, Mae had invited her visiting friend to attend and to meet the young minister there who knew the Bible so well.

Al spent a couple of hours with them discussing the Bible. The young man went on his way the next day, and Al never saw him again. But Mae began showing up at the evening meetings, and Al noticed her growing interest. He also noticed that she could sing well. When she turned in a card indicating an interest in Bible studies, Al found that he had been assigned this home to visit.

"The same home," he said to himself, remembering the place where some weeks earlier he had been treated so coldly. He rejoiced that now this home had opened for Bible studies. "Surely God works in mysterious ways," he recalled, putting it all together how through the coincidence of the young man's passing visit this interest had started. But it bothered him to see that still the mother and the other daughter cared nothing about the things he and Mae studied, always arranging to be absent about the time he arrived.

Conducting the song service at the tent meetings, Al watched the corner of the tent where Mae usually sat. "Wonder if she'll come tonight." His face would light up to see her take her accustomed place and join in the singing. If she missed an evening, Al found himself depressed. Does my depression represent a genuine concern for her soul?" he asked himself. "Or does it indicate only an emotional attraction?"

He also found himself opening up an account in the bank where she worked. Remarks made by his fellow workers alerted Albert that he had better be careful. "Seems you're spending a lot of time at the Sneesby home in prayer and Bible study," they would say. And, "Why do you find it necessary to go to the bank so often?"

Furthermore, Albert knew it wouldn't be fair to Mae to offer her any encouragement, in case her attendance at the meetings might only be her way of trying to get a husband. He prayed a lot about all this. He wanted her interest to be a genuine attraction to the truths being taught at the tent, and he wanted his interest in her to be simply a professional concern for her salvation.

But those flutterings in his heart made him question his own motives. "She can't be the one God has in mind for me," he would say. "We have nothing in common, except that we both have been brought up here in North Dakota, and we both like to sing."

Al noted concern as well as amusement on the faces of his fellow ministers, especially as his interest in Mae became more serious. "You might be bringing a Jezebel into the camp," they said one day. "Jezebel?" The possibility stunned him for a moment. Such talk only increased after Albert began inviting her to sing solos or join in duets at the meetings.

One night she showed up to sing wearing beads and a sleeveless dress, things Seventh-day Adventists did not wear. Al acted quickly. He noted that Mae had brought a light coat, but due to the warmness of the evening had taken it off. "For goodness sake, cover up," he said, picking up her coat and handing it back to her.

Mae sweetly complied, although at that point she had not been instructed on Adventist principles of dress. Al was impressed. Mae showed an admirable tolerance toward the viewpoints and practices of people who believed differently.

"I just hoped that a beautiful charm like that would never change," Albert confided in a close friend. "But can anybody possibly be as beautiful as that always?" he wondered to himself. Inwardly he wished for more of this kind of beauty in his own life and attitudes.

But still he had questions. She grew up in town and he in the country. Would that make them incompatible? What if he brought a girl like Mae home for his wife? "Boy, Albert's sure got a flapper this time." He could live with that, maybe, he reasoned. But he couldn't make a success of his ministry with a fashion model.

"She has more formal education than I do," he acknowledged. "What would that do to our marriage? Would she dominate me and try to push me into roles distasteful to me or out of harmony with my calling as a minister?"

Furthermore, never having had to endure poverty, could she live on a minister's salary? And always having known the security of a settled home, could she cope with the constant gypsy life of an itinerant evangelist? Albert could see potential conflict everywhere he looked.

Even if she did accept Seventh-day Adventist faith would she still have only a superficial knowledge of the church's beliefs? Would she be a stony-ground convert, soon falling away in time of temptation? And if she remained faithful, could she help him in giving Bible studies and in defending the faith against critics?

In Albert's estimation, Mrs. Sneesby's opposition showed up, too, as a serious threat to Mae's remaining faithful, even if she joined the Adventist Church at all. He observed that a close bond existed between mother and daughter. And he detected resentment from Mae's mother as well as from her sister against the intrusion of this eligible bachelor into their family circle.

But Albert frequently remembered his special text: "My thoughts are not your thoughts, neither are your ways my ways, saith the Lord." He took comfort from the assurance that as long as he kept his will surrendered to God's will and depended on His strength and wisdom, God would guide him in safe paths to fulfill his appointed part in Heaven's great plan.

Finally at the end of summer came the night for the final meeting. Up till then many had shown an interest, some having attended every meeting. But no one had yet decided for baptism. Albert watched from the platform as Evangelist Bresee made his last appeal. Albert watched and prayed. Would anybody stand and come forward?

Nobody stood. Then he saw Mae, all alone, get up and resolutely walk down the center aisle to the front. He could not restrain his tears. What courage! Her bold move was God's answer to all his prayers. God was saying to him: Of course, My son. She's the right one for you.

Albert felt a merciful release from tension after that. One evening a week or so following the baptism, Albert called at her home to make an appointment. He felt the time had come to let her know how he really felt. Mae had gone out for the evening, visiting at the home of some friends, but her mother relayed the message to her that Albert would be coming over. Mae too had been praying for guidance.

Driving to her house, Albert met her on the sidewalk as she made her way home. In his Ford they drove down a side street that led out into the countryside. There in the quiet of the evening beside a burning strawstack in an open field, Mae said Yes to Al's proposal of marriage. And together they committed themselves to God to walk side by side in His service.

Though their relationship so far had been brief, at this point neither Al nor Mae had the slightest doubt but that God had led them together. So they proceeded to make their engagement brief also, setting the wedding date for Thanksgiving Day. Al requested his conference president, Elder Meyer, to solemnize the wedding. Mae's mother consented to have the service in her living room and graciously prepared a delicious Thanksgiving dinner.

Into the beautiful simplicity, Al recalls, came a touch of unexpected harshness. Scarcely had the young couple swallowed their last bite of wedding cake, when Elder Meyer said, "Al, come on now; let's go."

"Go where?" Al wanted to know. Prior to this his president had not mentioned plans for going any place.

"I want to make some calls, and I want you to come with me."

Puzzled, Al dutifully accompanied his conference president and didn't get back to his bride till close to eleven that night. Albert says he was never able to figure that one out.

They began their honeymoon, which lasted just two

nights and one day between.

As soon as Elder Meyer released him, Al bundled his bride into his little one-passenger Ford and took off for a hotel in New Rockford, fifty miles away. The next day they drove on another two hundred miles or so to Al's farm home, where Mae fitted graciously into his family.

"The Lord led all the way," Albert says. "He made no mistake in putting Mae and me together. He kept me for her and her for me until we found each other." He thinks he probably gave some of his steel to her and she some of her velvet to him. From that beginning on Thanksgiving Day in 1924 until Mae's death in 1978, they worked as an efficient and harmonious team, preaching the gospel in word and song to thousands. Many years later Albert could still pray, "Thank You, Lord, for helping me find the right girl."

Elisabeth and Gottlieb Leiske.

Pauline, Albert, and Therisa Leiske at home. ☐Albert wearing Liberty Bell pin given to him by his fourth-grade teacher.

Albert as teenager. ☐ While teaching school at Turtle Lake in 1922, Albert at age 21 rents a room in the home of John Walker.

Mae Sneesby Leiske. ☐ The newlywed Albert at age 24.

Acting-attorney Leiske (left, facing camera) defends store-owner T. P. Neuens (right, in witness chair) in the court of Judge L. L. Moe (right) against the charge of violating a Sunday-closing law in Valley City, North Dakota, May 25, 1932

Evangelist's view of audience attending Leiske's first campaign in Denver, Colorado, opening May 3, 1933.

The "Bible Temple" in Greeley, Colorado in the July campaign of 1937. Standing with the Leiskes are the Harold Turners and the R. E. Finneys. Subject of tonight's lecture: "The Mark of the Beast."

Evangelistic team rejoices to see the first copies of *The Bible Temple Special* edition of a local newspaper in Loveland, Colorado on November 26, 1937. To the right of Leiske are singing evangelist Harold Turner and Mae.

After organizing a successful drive to raise $2,000 for materials and recruiting volunteers to build a new house, Evangelist Leiske hands a widow whose house had burned down in 1938 a check for ...

Many years later the Bishop and Mae returned with the author to visit the old Seventh-day Adventist church building on North Wahsatch Street, Colorado Springs, Colorado where Pastor Leiske served in 1943.

☐ Pastor Leiske in Oakes, North Dakota with son Bob and dog Bowser.

John Wimmer, who saw a telecast of the "American Religious Town Hall Meeting" (ARTHM), donated $70,000 to help establish a senior citizens' home in Twin Valley, North Dakota which became one of many such homes owned by ARTHM which finances the telecast.

Mother Superior challenges the Bishop for a change in the American Religious Town Hall Meeting plans. ☐ The author and Karol Baumeister share the duties of announcing on the "American Religious Town Hall Meeting" telecast.

The five founders of the American Religious Town Hall Meeting meet in the Bishop's home in St. Paul, Minnesota on December 5, 1952, to sign the original agreement. From left: Dr. Lloyd Gilmett, Dr. Mahlon W. Pomeroy, the Bishop, Dr. Ira

The five signatory founders celebrate the Town Hall's twenty-fifth anniversary in Dallas, February 20, 1977. As of this writing all five still live.

Pastor Robert Leiske displays a bottle of water he drew from the Jordan River at the traditional site of Jesus' baptism. To the

The Bishop often wields a light gavel. ☐ Father Damian Fandal elucidates a Roman Catholic position for Dr. Nelson and hundreds of thousands of viewers.

The Bishop stands before one of the thirteen retirement and nursing centers owned and operated by ARTHM, Inc., whose slogan is "Love makes the difference." ☐ The Bishop and Wana keep in shape on a custom bicycle built for two.

The president of ARTHM, Robert Leiske, visits with his father, the chairman of the board, at the elder's home on Dixie Lane in Dallas.

Made Good as Rookie Evangelist

"We thought he would never stop," Albert overheard Evangelist Bresee say to his associate Ben Scherr one evening in Devil's Lake after the evening meeting. That night Albert had preached after finally having been given the chance. "Why, he talked from Dan to Beersheba," the elder minister said.

Albert felt his hopes collapsing. "What chance is there for me?" he said to himself. He knew he had used too many texts in his sermon. And he had noticed people fidgeting in their seats. He had dearly wanted to measure up to his superiors' expectations. Now he despaired of ever succeeding as an evangelist. "Forty years looked like a long time to me then," he recalled later, "and I couldn't even see past year one."

But the older men laughed the matter off. "Don't worry," they said. "It all comes by practice."

Albert also remembered one of his favorite texts: "With God all things are possible." Mark 10:27. He looked it up again in his Bible and found it still there. He also found another promise that gave him the assurance he needed at that moment, a promise God had once made to another man facing forty years of ministry who also felt inadequate: "I will be with thy mouth, and teach thee what thou shall say." Exodus 4:12. Albert had faced closed doors before and had seen God work miracles, and he silently prayed, "Do it again, Lord, please; and do it for me, as You did for Moses."

The budding evangelist had gone on that winter and into the next summer with his year of internship, thankful for this opportunity for on-the-job training. The experience, however, made him realize his need for more schooling.

But how could he take time off and go back to college now that he had a wife to support? Here again he seemed to face a closed door. He and Mae hadn't even had enough money to get a wedding picture taken. Where would he get money for tuition?

But again God set a table in the wilderness. That fall, the beginning of the academic year 1925-26, Albert enrolled as a theological student in Union College, Lincoln, Nebraska.

Now Albert found himself burning the midnight oil just as his parents had done years before studying the Bible by the light of their kerosene lamps. He vowed to learn as many texts as his professor, W. W. Prescott, head of the Bible department, whose knowledge of the Bible made a deep impression on him.

"His biblical knowledge and sincere Christian attitudes," Albert says, "greatly influenced my life, my preaching, and my future." Prior to this time, Albert had already memorized many texts with their references. But during this year of study under Professor Prescott he came to know his Bible so well that he could turn to almost any text he needed without a moment's hesitation.

Albert, realizing that he also needed to improve his public speaking, took as many speech classes as he could. "I learned something of the value and power in a properly turned phrase," Albert recalls, "and I learned something of the great potentials of persuasion."

Nobody needed to prod Albert to do the class assignments. With a hunger that could not be satisfied, he took great gulping bites of knowledge and kept asking for more. The old urge for fun and pranks had to be sublimated to the serious creative pursuits more in harmony with his life purpose.

He began practicing the principles of public speaking he was learning. He arranged a series of noon meetings at the railroad yards in Havelock, a suburb of Lincoln—a student project in evangelism. Standing on a box, he would preach to the workmen as they sat eating their lunch beside the giant locomotives. Ever innovative, Albert spiced up the program by co-opting fellow students to do special musical features. One of the students, George Hutches, who later became president of the Michigan Conference, remembers that "the workers were fascinated by Albert's discussion and appeals; and they referred to him as another 'Billy Sunday.'"

The North Dakota Conference didn't have to twist Albert Leiske's arm in 1926 to get him to come back to his native state for full-time evangelism. "I loved North Dakota," Albert says, "and actually felt hurt when eight years later the conference president didn't see light in my staying on longer and approved my transfer to Missouri."

During those eight years Albert traveled with Mae throughout the state as an itinerant evangelist. In the tradition of the circus and chautauqua, Leiske often held his meetings in a large tent with a seating capacity upwards of 1000. Before the time of motor homes, the evangelistic team often lived behind the big tent in small family tents. Albert remembers sometimes occupying the same tent with the associate evangelist, with only a curtain between the two couples.

In winter, of course, they resorted to more permanent quarters, both for living as well as for holding the meetings.

Having grown up in North Dakota, neither Albert nor Mae suffered any great discomfort from the sub-zero winters, finding it natural to take in stride what others might have found intolerable. They loved the hardy people who braved the elements to come to the meetings under such forbidding circumstances.

At one place Mae took a hot-water bottle to bed one night

to help keep her warm; it froze solid before morning light. It reminded Albert of the joke people told about milking cows in North Dakota—the milk would freeze to ice right while the farmers milked, and the streams would stand up in the pail like straws.

Sometimes it would be so cold Albert could not sleep. Then texts would come to his mind, as though God were speaking to him. Such experiences often followed a meeting when a question had been asked which he could not answer, at least not to his own satisfaction. "So I would pray about it," he recalls, "and ask the Lord to help me to know how to answer that question."

During the night, then, Albert would have a dream, the whole meeting being reenacted in his subconscious mind. "There in the darkness," he says, "the Lord would give me different passages and the places where I could find them."

Ever seeking ways to increase attendance at his meetings, Albert designated one entire evening each week, usually a Saturday night, as "cross-examining-the-preacher" night. "That night," Albert explains, "I had to be prepared to answer questions from the floor for an hour, sort of like a President's news conference. The people loved it. It gave them their opportunity to talk back to the preacher, often with evident relish if they could make him hum and haw over the answer and could see his face turn red."

One night a woman evidently intended to occupy the whole evening. When Albert opened the meeting for questions, she popped up with her first one. After the answer she immediately asked a second question, then a third, and so on. "I saw hands up all over the place," Albert says, "but this lady kept standing there firing one question after another."

At length he interrupted, "Lady, would you let me ask a question?"

"Yes."

"How do we know there will be no women in heaven?"

She replied that she had never read that in the Bible and asked Albert for the text.

He gave the reference, Revelation 8:1, and asked her to read it.

"'There was silence in heaven about the space of half an hour,'" she read. Then with a puzzled expression, said, "I don't get it."

"Read it again," Leiske suggested.

At last the import of what Albert was trying to get across dawned on her, and she sank silently back into her chair.

"It just took the wind out of her sails," he recalls. "But it saved the evening for the rest of the audience." Feeling sorry for her, though, Albert apologized afterward for the embarrassment he had caused her.

Albert used a perennial question in those days, "Is it wrong for a woman to have short hair?" to direct people's minds to "weightier matters of the law." But in answering he went through a humorous little act. Putting his hand to his bald head, he would repeat the key word *hair* a couple of times with a quizzical look in his eye. The audience would begin to chuckle. Then he would simply get rid of the question, usually to everyone's satisfaction, by saying, "Boy, if it takes hair to get a fellow into heaven, I'm in one awful fix, aren't I?" That quip would bring the house down.

Albert and Mae went all over North Dakota, conducting evangelistic meetings in small towns and country communities, as well as in the larger cities. Places little known outside the state show up in the handbills—like Antelope, Oakes, Hebron, and Lisbon.

When Albert, with his evangelistic team, drove into Oakes one summer day, he looked out over the ripening grainfields surrounding the little town and said, "Well, in a few weeks this town and community will be different."

"In what way?" one of his associates asked.

"There will be a Seventh-day Adventist church here," he replied with his characteristic confidence in God.

And, sure enough, it happened, just as he said.

In Hebron, a largely German community, the minister in charge, John Seibel, preached in German, and Albert led the music in German. During the day, however, as Albert and Mae called on homes, they found many people who spoke English and who wanted religious services in English. These people had a church building but no preacher. So they invited Albert to preach every Sunday in their church, and Mae would sing. Thus they preached and sang their way into the hearts of these English-speaking people, resulting in several of them accepting the Sabbath truth.

Thus in place after place, Albert and Mae experienced the inner glow that comes to Christian workers in seeing lives transformed by the grace of God and whole companies worshiping their Creator on His holy day. And the churches they established proved sound and steadfast, a tribute to this couple's thoroughness in leading their converts into a saving relationship with Jesus Christ. Ten years later a new conference president, Elder George Hutches, commented after visiting throughout the state, "I am overwhelmed by the number I find who trace their original connection to the Adventist faith to Albert and Mae's ministry."

All of this led to a climactic day in Albert's life in the summer of 1929.

"Good news for you, Honey!" Albert shouted, bursting into the house and waving a letter from the conference president. All ears and eyes, Mae dropped everything to join her husband in reading what the letter said: "The conference committee has voted to ordain you to the gospel ministry. The date, June 26, at camp meeting."

"Can you believe it?" Albert said, "and from Elder Meyer, of all people!" Albert couldn't help reflecting on that time when he trudged along with this same minister making some calls until about eleven o'clock on his wedding night. "I wonder if he himself doesn't find it hard to believe that the greenhorn worker he knew back there could have developed to the stage of ordination."

After the first burst of elation had passed, Albert felt the seriousness of the news, sensing the weightier responsibility that would now rest upon him. "'Elder,' they will call me now," he mused. "No longer a 'novice,' but a 'bishop,' as Paul puts it in his first letter to Timothy."

Also a deep sense of gratitude came over them both as they reviewed briefly the way God had led them since that day of despondency when Albert himself had despaired of ever measuring up as an evangelist. And together they dropped to their knees beside the kitchen table and rededicated their lives to the Master's service.

"Thank You, Lord," Albert said, "for fulfilling Your promise so abundantly. How true it is that all things are possible with You. And indeed Your ways are higher than ours, higher than the heavens are above the earth."

Took Role of Attorney

"Your Honor, if the state's attorney objects to procedure, I will just lay the Bible aside and quote it."

Albert Leiske, the evangelist, spoke these words in the role of Albert Leiske, the attorney, standing that day, May 25, 1932, in the courtroom of Judge I. J. Moe in Valley City, North Dakota.

The story had its beginning several weeks earlier, when the Leiske evangelistic team had moved into Valley City and had begun a series of meetings in a large tent. As Albert remembers developments that summer, the meetings progressed with mounting interest, culminating in city-wide agitation when he advertised his lecture on who changed the Sabbath.

In his handbill Albert had promised to pinpoint the culprit, using the Bible and history as supporting evidence. Apparently feeling threatened, a priest had sent a note to Albert stating that if he knew what was good for him, he would change his subject.

During several nights immediately preceding that lecture, Albert took full advantage of the opportunity to heighten interest in that evening's topic. Reading the note to his audience, he admitted that it naturally caused him to think twice before going ahead. But, said he, intimidation could not keep him from preaching God's Word, and he planned to stick to his subject.

So of course the next night people would come wondering

if his knees would be shaking. And as the night came closer, more people would come out just to see who would win in this battle of nerves.

Albert learned of counter-threats by a group supporting him, warning potential troublemakers against any attempt to harm the preacher or damage the tent. All this fomentation had so contributed to the taking of sides that hardly anyone in the city remained neutral.

Evangelist Leiske could not identify or fully describe the driving force in his soul when the night for the controversial lecture finally arrived. He recognized the elements of the past as part of it—urges that motivated him as a boy, as a grade-school orator, as a high school senior. Always an aggressive champion of American freedoms and human rights, he had set his course. This commitment, plus his ordination vows to fearlessly preach God's Word, left him no options but to go ahead with his presentation as planned.

"When I hung up my chart on Revelation 13," Albert recalls, "excitement in the packed tent that night had reached a high pitch."

He remembers that evening's service as a soul-moving revival meeting. People saw the issues, and some dared to line up on God's side, among them a Mr. T. P. Neuens.

"What shall I do now?" Neuens had asked Albert when he lost his job because of his refusal to work on the Sabbath.

"Why not open your own grocery store on Sunday?" Albert had suggested. Neuens had had experience in merchandising, especially in the grocery business. So with Albert's encouragement, he opened a local corner grocery store on East Main Street.

"Just close Friday night before sunset," Albert counseled. "Then open again Saturday night after sunset and remain open all day Sunday. Put a notice on the door to that effect, and that in itself will be a witness to your faith."

It worked well at first, with Mr. Neuens doing a good business. But when the Lord's Day Alliance got word of this new grocery store open on Sundays, they saw a threat to the morals of the community. Also Mr. Neuens's thriving trade began to raise the cry of "unfair practices" on the part of his competitors.

Albert heard from Mr. Neuens about these rumblings, and the two of them kept a close eye on fresh developments as they took place. It seemed fairly certain that sooner or later things would come to a crisis.

Albert went to the store to bolster his friend's courage. "Don't worry," Albert said as they sat talking. "Remember, God has His own ways of handling problems like these, and we have His word that 'all things are possible' with Him."

"But the wholesalers might boycott me." Mr. Neuens got up and paced the floor. "They'll find some way to put the squeeze on me."

"Let's pray about it," Albert suggested. So in the produce room at the back of the store beside a sack of potatoes, with egg crates, a stalk of bananas, and other grocery items stacked around them, they knelt together and sought divine intervention in the serious threat Mr. Neuens faced.

Shaking his friend's hand as he left, Albert said, "God may let another fiery-furnace episode develop out of all this. Who knows? If He does, you can rest assured He will use the occasion to proclaim His truth and His power so that everybody in this city and far beyond it will know about the true Sabbath and about His power to overrule the designs of those who try to oppose His will."

Before the next Sunday came around, news leaked out that officials of the Retailers Association and the Lord's Day Alliance had connived together in a strategy session.

Rumors had it that a decision had been reached to have Mr. Neuens arrested if he opened his store for business again on Sunday.

"Well, the worst has happened," Neuens phoned Albert on Friday. "They came this morning and served notice on me."

"What kind of notice?" Albert inquired. "What law have you violated?"

"Well, it seems," Neuens replied, "they peered into the ordinances on the town books and found a Sunday-closing law tailored to their designs. It specifies that to sell groceries after ten o'clock on Sunday morning constitutes a crime."

Albert couldn't believe his ears. Wasn't North Dakota still a part of free America? All the accumulated crusading spirit against intolerance in his system exploded in indignation. What blatant interference with rights constitutionally guaranteed to law-abiding citizens trying to make an honest living in an honorable, decent way! He remembered his vow made in his youth, "If I ever get a chance to hit this thing, I'll hit it hard." Maybe his chance had come.

"Go ahead and open on Sunday as usual," Albert advised his friend. "If you get hauled into court, I'll take care of you." Neuens promised to keep Albert informed and hung up.

"Whew!" Albert exclaimed, wiping the sweat from his forehead. "What have I gotten myself into now?" With no legal training, how could he "take care" of Neuens? He braced himself for battle. If worse came to worst, he would have to do a lot of boning up on the laws and court procedures.

Albert stayed close to his telephone Sunday morning, waiting for a call from his friend. Sure enough, about fifteen minutes after ten his phone rang, with Neuens on the line.

"It's happened," he heard Neuens say. "The president of the Retailers Association came in this morning and bought a few little things."

Albert kept listening as the story unfolded. It seems that the law specified that a sale actually had to be made before a citation could be issued. But just as soon as Neuens had taken the money, the man hurried to the nearest phone to inform the police.

The next day Neuens had to stand trial before Police

Magistrate R. J. McDonald, who fined him $10 and costs for a first offense. But Albert, representing Neuens, asked for a full jury trial.

At first the magistrate refused Leiske's right to speak for the defendant. But when both the defendant and Albert insisted that the defendant had retained Leiske as his attorney, he heard Albert's request and granted it.

So the court set May 25, 1932, as the day for the trial, the case to be heard by Judge I. J. Moe. The state's attorney would prosecute the case on behalf of the city.

Leiske saw himself as David down in the ravine looking up at the raging Goliath. To find some stones for this sling, he burned some midnight oil reading case law dealing with Sunday-closing ordinances and studying legal procedures.

At the same time Albert continued his regular devotions every morning. In fact, the approaching crisis seemed to demand more time than usual for prayer and consecration. He reminded Neuens that "all things work together for good to them that love God" and that God sets "a table in the wilderness" for people who get into trouble while acting "according to God's purpose" Romans 8:28.

First the jury had to be selected, six members by the prosecuting attorney and six by Albert. When the judge called the court to order, the prosecution and the defense each briefed the jury regarding the issue.

The prosecuting attorney examined the witnesses for the plaintiff. Then Albert cross-examined them. "Did you say you were in Mr. Neuens's place of business on Sunday morning?" "Yes," said the witness, who was also the plaintiff. "What was your business at Mr. Neuens's general store that morning?" "Shopping for groceries," he replied. Leiske pursuing further, "What groceries did you purchase that Sunday morning?" "I purchased bananas, potatoes, and baloney." "How much baloney?" asked Leiske. "A dime's worth." A voice from the rear of the courtroom shouted, "That's too much baloney!"

As the defense attorney, Albert put Mr. Neuens on the stand and asked him to tell the court how he observed the Sabbath and why he kept his store open on Sunday.

Mr. Neuens gave the court an outline of what he believed regarding Sabbath observance, Albert remembers, "so much so that the Methodist minister sitting in the courtroom said afterward, 'I was not afraid that Leiske would not win the case, but I was afraid that everybody in the courtroom would be keeping the Sabbath by the time he got through.'"

"This is a matter of church and state," Albert summed up before the jury, "and it is a question of whether people have a right in America to believe what they want to believe and then to be protected by the law of our government and by our courts."

Albert cited the Holy Bible from Genesis to Revelation as the only creed of the Seventh-day Adventist Church and stated that this creed requires members of the church to work six days and rest on the seventh. To substantiate his argument, he proceeded to read the fourth commandment of the Decalogue (Exodus 20:8-11).

The state's attorney jumped to his feet. "Your Honor," he said, "I object to his using Scripture as evidence in this court!" The judge tried to overrule in Leiske's favor, but the prosecutor continued to object. At this point Leiske requested permission to at least quote from the Bible.

Given permission, he quoted the fourth commandment by heart. "This is a religious law found in the Bible," Leiske pointed out to the jury, "an obligation man owes to God. And, according to our national constitution, there should be no interference from the state or any court in religious matters." "I maintain," he went on, "that the defendant has the guaranteed right to live his religion unmolested."

"Mr. Neuens has fought in the armed forces, and we have given our lives and our all for these human rights and these religious freedoms in America. We are not about to surrender at this point. We would rather die than surrender these rights. And I am asking the jury to find the defendant not guilty."

When the time for the jury's verdict came near, Albert felt calm, fully believing that God had the whole matter in His care. The news of the trial was headlined by leading newspapers throughout the state. If a victory would be won, everybody would know about it, and God's name would be glorified.

About ten o'clock that night, Albert received a phone call from the bailiff, who said, "It looks like we have a hung jury. One man thinks Neuens ought to be found guilty for not keeping the Sabbath day."

"Hold them a little longer," Albert requested, "and call me back in five minutes or so."

Hanging up the receiver, Albert said to Mae, "There's one fellow we haven't convinced. Let's just kneel down and ask the Lord to change that man's mind and bring in a not guilty."

They had not finished praying when the phone rang again. "They've decided now," the bailiff said. "They're bringing in a unanimous decision—not guilty."

"What a victory for the cause of God that day in North Dakota!" Albert penned in his diary. And the law of the state, he observes, was changed to read: "It is of sufficient defense for servile labor on the first day of the week if it can be shown that the accused uniformly observes another day as holy time."

T. P. Neuens went on selling groceries on Sunday.

And Albert Leiske, the attorney, went back to the more accustomed role of Albert Leiske, the evangelist, his heart rejoicing in the goodness and power of God.

Entered Big-League Evangelism

"I'm the Grand Dragon of the state of North Dakota," the man told Albert one night, stepping forward out of the shadows at the back of the tent, "and I've come to give you some advice."

Albert was continuing his series of meetings in Valley City in 1932.

"Well," Albert replied, "I have often preached about the dragon, but this is the first time I have ever met him. What can I do for you?"

At that point Albert couldn't be sure about this stranger's intentions. He had heard rumors of possible violence; one fellow reportedly had been seen with a huge monkey wrench in his hand. Or perhaps this fellow was a nut and perhaps dangerous.

"Tomorrow," the Grand Dragon went on to say, "a car will come for you at two o'clock. My counsel would be that you follow orders and directions." Then he faded back into the shadows and disappeared, leaving an astounded Albert standing beside the tent.

At two the following day—just as promised—the Leiskes heard a rap on their tent door and a quiet voice saying, "We have come for you." Mae refused to stay behind.

The car took them out into the country about four miles, across a large open field, up a hill, and into a grove of trees. There they found the Grand Dragon with a group of robed fellow Klansmen waiting to receive them.

The group quickly assured them that they meant them no harm. "We only want to protect you," they said. They too had heard the rumors. They too had seen the fellow with the monkey wrench. "We thought you were in danger, and we felt you ought to tell us who you are and how you stand on the Roman question."

On the handbill they had noticed a lecture about Rome and America advertised for that Sunday night. Which should control the United States? the handbill asked. The KKK had heard rumblings of possible trouble when this topic would be presented.

Albert remembers this strange incident as one of God's providences during his years in big-time evangelism. That night he spoke to a standing-room-only audience, with 300 sheet-clad Klansmen patroling outside the tent. When the crowd had all left, Leiske saw a monkey wrench left behind on a seat in the third row. Whoever left it or whoever intended to use it, he never discovered.

Crowds—how to get bigger and better crowds? Albert was willing to try almost any publicity stunt—conventional or otherwise. He knew that before anyone would ever make a decision for Christ, he would have to hear Christ's invitation. And before a person would stop and listen, someone would have to get that person's attention.

Guided by this philosophy, Albert, though gifted by God with a voice like a bullhorn, began using the public address system, in those days still a novelty.

Shortly after the Valley City meetings, Albert received a call from the Missouri Conference to conduct meetings there, beginning in the tiny town of Livonia. Most of his potential audience lived on the surrounding farms.

Setting up a public address with outdoor speakers, he broadcast periodic news bulletins, during the day announced topics for his evening meetings, and played sacred records. "The Lord furnished a turntable for me in the wilderness," he reflects.

This method rewarded him with audiences that far out-numbered Livonia's population. "It was not unusual," he recalls, "to have a thousand people out for an evening meeting." Farmers in town to shop during the day heard the broadcasts and carried the word back to friends and neighbors.

Not so much as an allurement for crowds, but as a method for getting decisions, Albert found literature highly effective. Adapting a fairly common technique, he began a circulating library. He used three books—*The Repairing of Sam Brown* by Robert Thurber, *The Marked Bible* by Charles Taylor, and *The Last Warning Message* by Charles Everson.

"I had boxes full of these books," Leiske says. People would read the first one, then return it and take the second. By the time they read Everson's book, Albert and his team pressed for a decision. The plan proved to be a tremendous reinforcement.

For his crusades in Colorado, Leiske had a portable tabernacle built, not only as a place to hold meetings but also as a novel structure to attract attention. "It was designed," he explains, "so that we could haul the whole thing on the highways without a permit, the upright boards in each section being a couple of inches short of the critical eight-foot length.

"We would come blitzing into town with this nonde-script beast loaded into a semitrailer, just like a Barnum and Bailey circus coming to town," he says. "Construction on a prearranged lot would begin at once, while people stood around gawking and trying to figure out what kind of a contraption it would be." Just the guessing game itself constituted excellent advertising.

"It looked like a million dollars all up," he says, "the paneled walls all blow-torched and varnished, and the gracefully sloped canvas top." A group of workers, under the trained leadership of Harold Turner, Leiske's longtime associate, could assemble it in a matter of hours like an oversize Tinker Toy. In Grand Junction the ripples of speculation reached the labor-union officials who sent out two representatives to investigate. "Who's putting up this building?" they asked Turner. "Are you using union labor?" Turner sent them to Leiske.

"What union is putting this structure up?" they asked.

"The Central Union," Albert told them. "Their head-quarters are in Lincoln, Nebraska."

"Oh," the spokesman said, only half satisfied. "We have to go back and look it up."

So they returned to their office and searched the files. But by the time they discovered that the Central Union was not a bona fide labor organization and returned for more information, the tabernacle had already been set up.

This Grand Junction tabernacle series began in April of 1939, when the temperatures at night on the western slope still dropped to near freezing. "We had a problem about heating," Albert recalls. "To care for this need we installed gas blowers, with vents that went right through the canvas."

About the first day of the series, the city manager called on Albert, bringing the fire marshal with him. "You have to build chimneys for the stack," he said. "We cannot allow the smokestack to go right through the canvas."

Albert cited other places where his practice had been allowed. But the men wouldn't budge. "We will have to close you down," they said. "You do not have a regulation chimney."

So Albert went to the city office and took out a thirty-day permit. Then he appealed to his nightly audiences for the necessary funds to buy the bricks and build the chimneys, raising about $600.

"I bought the bricks," he says, "and poured the foundation for one chimney." But by then the weather had warmed up enough that they no longer needed heat. So they dismantled the gas blowers, returned the bricks to the dealer, and saved the conference $600 on the evangelistic budget.

Albert also employed the "closed-door" decoy or "sneak preview." He would issue tickets a week in advance for a specific upcoming lecture, stipulating that admission for that night would be allowed by ticket only, one person per ticket. Thus he took advantage of the natural curiosity and desire to "get in" on something exclusive. On those nights he had to turn many away who came hoping to get in without the required ticket.

With another technique, Albert would focus public attention on a political dignitary who would come on a particular night and serve as guest speaker. Albert's background and temperament had equipped him with the ability to hobnob with people in the higher echelons and to be accepted by them as an equal.

Governor Ed Johnson of Colorado, later U.S. senator from that state, for example, considered Albert Leiske a close personal friend. At a banquet once at the Porter Hospital in Denver he told a fellow guest sitting next to him, as they both noticed Leiske present at another table, "I have attended some of his meetings, and he comes to see me when he's in Denver. He is one of my favorite people."

Leiske once invited Johnson, senator then, to appear on his program at Greeley. He requested the senator to address the audience on the topic of religious liberty. The occasion provided a natural opening to attract the mayor and a number of other dignitaries from the city to attend also.

Knowing that the enclosure would not hold everyone, Albert issued tickets for reserved seating inside, but he invited the general public to the non-reserved area outside. In order to accommodate the huge crowd, his helpers had to enclose the entire lot in a tent wall, and even then people competed for standing room. Albert asked Senator Johnson to speak on American freedoms, the dignity of human rights, and tolerance among men for each other's beliefs.

Occasionally religious prejudice would assert itself

within a community, barring Albert from advertising his meetings in local newspapers. But his crusading spirit would not let him take such a refusal lying down. He kept remembering his vow to hit such prejudicial actions hard.

In Boulder, Colorado, he published his own newspaper. In fact this idea worked so well that he did this in other places too, where newspaper advertising was not closed to him. Sometimes with the cooperation of the publisher, he would take over one complete daily issue of the local newspaper.

In the Boulder crusade, Leiske drew the governor into his orbit, again also bringing in a bevy of local dignitaries. To publicize the event, he brought out on November 26, 1937, *The Bible Temple Special*. Across the front page he splashed the headline in fifty-six point (nearly an inch high) bold type: "Boulder to Hear Governor Ammons and Leiske." And he displayed a twelve-inch by four-column picture of the governor.

On this attention-getting front page Albert informed his readers about the meeting, a "closed-door" lecture on Sunday night. By press time, he let his readers know, 1200 people had already stopped by the office to make sure of admittance, adding, "There seems to be a rush for tickets."

In Montrose, Colorado, Albert hired "the devil" to picket his meetings. "I had him picket me for a week or so, pacing back and forth in front of my tabernacle."

In a now-it-can-be-told reflection, Albert tells how he planned this publicity stunt in total secrecy, not even letting his wife or associates in on it. He wanted it to seem like the real thing happening. In a radio talk the previous day he capitalized on what he alone knew would take place by making a prophecy.

"I have received word," he announced, "that the devil is very displeased and that he is going to be at the tabernacle tomorrow evening."

The next night on the sidewalk outside the tabernacle

strode a determined-looking character with a pitchfork over his shoulders and a long tail trailing behind. He wore a red body-length suit, including a mask for his face with two big horns. As he paced back and forth, he kept repeating, "I object to Leiske's lectures. He is stealing my sheep."

Some of the church members objected to this method of advertising as too sensational. They even called the conference president and reported the matter.

"But it brought the crowds to hear the truth," counters Leiske. "The tabernacle was packed. And it got the whole city talking about the meetings."

Albert Leiske became known as a debater, but he denies using the debating technique as a publicity stunt to get people to come to his meetings. In fact, he says he refused to debate during the designated duration of the series, realizing that a debate would arouse contention, incite ill will, and create an atmosphere unfavorable to calm and Spirit-directed consideration of the truths being presented.

"But," he says, "I considered debate helpful after the regular series for a stipulated period—a sort of additional campaign for reaffirming or confirming new believers or adding others still in the balance." And even then, Leiske points out, he insisted that the debate be conducted in a strictly parliamentary manner, with a judge appointed to preside.

Under those conditions Leiske once accepted a challenge to debate in Mercedes, Texas, his opponent being a Church of Christ minister named O'Dowd. The proposition was that the Seventh-day Adventist Church was of the devil. One night O'Dowd would affirm the proposition and Leiske deny; the next night Leiske would affirm the contrary position and O'Dowd deny. Everything was set up according to the rules of debate, with a secretary taking it all down in shorthand.

O'Dowd led off the first night. A large audience filled the auditorium. The judge sat on the platform to the right of the podium, and the secretary sat down front, pad in hand to take notes. "You could feel a certain tenseness in the room," Leiske remembers, "and understandably so. A lot of those people had just recently accepted the Adventist faith, and they naturally felt somewhat threatened and fearful." Quite a number of them had left O'Dowd's church, a fact which added to the tenseness.

Instead of using the Bible to support his statements, O'Dowd used a book written by a former Seventh-day Adventist minister, the Reverend D. M. Canright, turning to pages where he had inserted slips of paper as markers. He had it all organized, methodically listing his points according to Canright. For forty-five minutes he quoted from Canright's book, introducing his arguments by repeating often, "Canright has this to say."

"But while he was talking," Albert says, "the Holy Spirit impressed me that I should address this minister as 'Reverend O'Dowd.'" Albert didn't understand why he should do that, but he did it.

Immediately his opponent jumped to his feet, saying to the judge, "Your Honor, I have an objection!"

"State your objection."

"The Church of Christ believes that ministers have no business calling themselves 'Reverend.' God only is reverend and holy." And he quoted a supporting text, the only time up to then that he had used the Bible. He went so far in his objection as to state that any man who calls himself "Reverend" is of the devil."

"That's right," Leiske replied, "I yield, Your Honor."

"Now," Leiske proceeded, "we want to see where Brother O'Dowd got his information that the Adventist Church is of the devil. Could I have that book?"

On the cover of the book in letters large enough to be seen by people on the first few rows, and certainly plain enough for the judge to see, was the author's name—"Reverend D. M. Canright."

"I knew then," Albert says, "why the Holy Spirit had impressed me to call O'Dowd 'Reverend.'" The man had allowed himself to indirectly label the author of his source a "devil." And the trap had sprung shut.

"You could have heard a pin drop at that electric moment," Albert recalls. Then he broke the tense silence by walking over to his opponent and saying, "Brother O'Dowd, don't you think you ought to surrender to Christ and preach the gospel, instead of going around preaching from the devil's book?"

"Since the devil is a liar," Leiske went on to say, "I'm not going to answer to the devil, and so I'll just preach a sermon on the judgment."

There the debate ended, with the faith of any who might have been in doubt fully confirmed.

Looking back on his experience in evangelism, Albert Leiske sees the practice that it gave him in presenting his thoughts logically and convincingly and the opportunity it gave him in meeting people of all faiths and in high positions. It was divinely ordained preparation for the greater ministry God had in mind for him. And he says, "Thank You, Lord, for the way You put it all together."

Used Zoom-Lens Focus

For all of Albert's emphasis on large attendance, the bottom line was always the salvation of individual lost souls. Everything focused on that.

In a series of meetings in Delta, Colorado, Albert preached to a one-man audience winning him to Christ. He knew about the audience inside the tabernacle, one lady in particular already a member of the Adventist Church. But he didn't know about her husband sitting outside alone in his car, intending to shoot the preacher.

After a week of meetings, Leiske heard a rap on his office door in the tabernacle and in walked this man, a person he had never seen before.

"Mr. Leiske," he said, "you do not know me, but I have been trying to kill you every night this past week. But last night I made up my mind instead to beg you to baptize me and make me a member of your church."

Then he spilled out the whole story of his intense hostility toward his wife's religion and his decision to take his wrath out on her preacher. So he had come each night with a loaded gun, waiting outside and listening to the sermon that came booming out through the canvas roof. At length he had yielded to the conviction that came to him. Now he wanted to be baptized.

Albert dropped everything else the next Monday morning and went out to this man's farm to go over the major points of

Seventh-day Adventist doctrine with him. He wanted to make sure that the man thoroughly understood the step he intended to take.

The man's wife, not knowing that her husband had had a change of heart, stood flabbergasted at seeing the Adventist preacher at her front door. Only with great reluctance did she let him in.

Albert, knowing what she did not, could hardly wait to witness the joy that would come to her, who had prayed so long for this day.

"Really?" she exclaimed, grabbing her husband around the waist and dancing him around the dining table. "Are your really going to be baptized? Glory! Hallelujah!"

Remembering another series of meetings, in Marshall, Missouri, Albert still wakes up at night in a sweat over that tragic scene.

A man and wife had been regularly attending the meetings. The wife, Albert learned later, was obsessively jealous of her husband. An attractive middle-aged nurse, a single lady, had also been coming.

"One night I made an altar call," Albert painfully reflects, "and it so happened that the lady and her husband knelt opposite each other, while the nurse knelt alongside the husband. Well, the wife opened her eyes during prayer and saw the nurse kneeling next to her husband. Right there during the prayer at the altar she jumped up and hollered out, 'My Lord, now I've seen everything!'"

She stormed out of the meeting and a short time later left her home and her husband. She reported the matter to the town mayor, describing what happened at the meeting as unspeakable wickedness—her husband "making love" to this nurse right there at the altar.

"Not only did that husband lose his wife in that distressing fracas," Albert sadly concludes, "but we lost a precious soul and maybe several other souls in the aftermath before we could regroup and get things stabilized again."

Another experience he wishes he could forget took place in Loveland, Colorado, where another tragedy may have caused the loss of souls.

An Adventist lady, rather overweight, had at the close of the first meeting planted herself in the entrance of the tabernacle, bunching up the people inside the door instead of allowing them to file out as they normally did. Albert made his way to the back as fast as he could.

There he found this overweight and overzealous believer blocking the exit in her desire to help the evangelist win souls. She had waited so long for the people of her town to hear the full message. She had been terribly disappointed that the evangelist at that first meeting had missed his golden opportunity by giving only a tiny bit of truth.

She stood in the doorway with both hands up, saying, "No, no, people, you are not going home yet. The evangelist really did not give you enough of the truth. I will tell you about the 'mark of the beast' we are facing." Trying her best to give the whole message in two minutes, she succeeded only in making her captive audience angry.

Albert didn't want to insult her, yet he knew that already her fanaticism had prejudiced some from ever coming back again. He had to act quickly and decisively. Finally he got her out of the doorway and on her way home. Again, Albert recalls, "We had a hard time regrouping and bringing the people back to the meetings."

In Detroit, Albert kept noticing a policeman in his congregation. This man came nearly every Sabbath with his wife and two children. "But he never could take his stand for the truth." Finally Albert decided to give this policeman the "shock treatment." "Some people need that," he points out. He told the family that he planned to visit them on a certain Sunday morning and that he wanted the whole family together.

"Now," he said at the meeting, "we're together today to help Dad make up his mind to be baptized. We want to discuss this matter and take a vote."

He asked the children to speak first. "What do you think?" he asked Mary. "Dad is getting up in years. How do you feel about this matter?" After she spoke, John gave his opinion. Then Albert asked Mother what she thought. She of course heartily agreed with the children, saying, "Dad ought to make up his mind and go with his family to the kingdom."

Next Albert circled a Sabbath date on the calendar and asked someone in the room to move that Dad be baptized on that Sabbath. So Mary moved it, and her brother seconded it. Now the pastor asked Dad to speak to the motion. "Are you in harmony with it? And if not, why not?"

Too overwhelmed at first to say anything, the policeman sat there, quivering and with tears in his eyes. At last he said, "How can I hold back on my family? Why, I wouldn't disappoint them for anything. Sure, I'll be baptized." Then they all voted. Including Dad. And the policeman became a baptized member at long last.

In Longmont, Colorado, as Albert began speaking one evening on the importance of Bible study and the reliability of the Bible as the Word of God, a cowboy, not bothering to remove his big western hat, strode down the center aisle. To Albert he looked as though he could mean trouble. He sat and listened for a few minutes, then jumped to his feet and shouted, "That's all baloney! Just plain bunk!"

Albert quietly let everyone settle, then said, "You're right, brother, absolutely correct. Anything I say is all bunk, but what God says in this Book is the truth—from beginning to end. And you had better let it stick to your ribs. Right under where I stand is a baptistry. And if you aren't careful, you'll be the first fellow under the water right here before all these people."

Suddenly speechless, the fellow grabbed his hat from his head and sat on it the rest of the evening, intently taking in every word of the sermon.

At the end of the sermon the cowboy bolted out. He never came back. But Albert hopes that maybe the sermon he heard that night may have started him studying the Bible and may have eventually led him into the fold of the True Shepherd.

In Denver, Albert saw a similar scene played this time with a drunk. It happened that one night when no meeting had been scheduled Albert and an associate found a man drunk in the entryway of the tabernacle.

"What are you doing here?" they asked.

"I came . . . to attend . . . the meeting."

Albert opened the door, turned on the lights, and gave a little talk, just for that one man. Here again Albert doesn't know the outcome. "But I considered it a big part of my ministry to help people who had messed up their lives or who faced sorrow or a big problem, and often it would be a lone individual."

People meant everything. Albert saw them as God's property and himself as God's appointed one to help them, to do for them whatever needed to be done to win them for Christ.

Albert's focus on the individual in his ministry began while he was still a student in Union College. During the time he conducted those noon-hour meetings for the railway men in that Lincoln suburb, one of those men lost his wife. Albert at once responded to the need, visiting the family in their home and conducting the funeral. He remembers the funeral as particularly sad, conducted right there in the home. He can still see the silent father and the two wide-eyed little children sitting there before him. The children apparently couldn't understand why everyone was crying, saying their mother ought only to wake up.

After the service Albert sat down with them, setting one on each knee. Drawing them close, he explained that their mother would indeed wake up again some day. Jesus would come and open her eyes, and she would hug and kiss them once again. Till then, they must try to help Daddy by being brave and obedient, so that then Jesus came they too would be ready to go to heaven with their mommy and daddy.

Later he held Bible studies with the father, and the children grew up to be faithful members of the Adventist Church.

In whatever community Albert lived, he developed a reputation as the minister to call if anyone got into trouble, became sick, or died. He preached many funeral sermons, and he always found time in his busy schedule to visit the sick.

Albert enjoyed "setting tables in the wilderness" for anyone who had come to the end of his tether. He never forgot how God had used others to help him and his family many times during his growing-up years. He felt he owed a big debt to anyone in need, for Jesus said, "Inasmuch as ye have done it unto one of the least of these my brethren, ye have done it unto me."

Once he found one of these "brethren" hitchhiking on a desert highway in southern California. The road stretched out for miles, and the sun's heat radiating from the dry sandy wasteland rippled above the desert floor. Here nature had turned the wilderness into a fiery furnace.

Albert wondered why a man would be hitchhiking in such weather and along such a lonely road. First he passed him by. Then, studying him in his rearview mirror, he decided to risk picking him up. He turned around and went back still studying him keenly. Seeing real anguish on the man's face, he made another U-turn, stopped, and let the stranger in.

In obvious relief and joy the almost exhausted hiker stumbled into the car frothing at the mouth and nearly dying of thirst. Albert offered him a juicy orange from a bag of oranges he had in the car, and the fellow almost swallowed it whole.

"What are you doing out here?" Albert asked him.

"Looking over some land I bought," he replied. "My car got stuck in the sand."

Before Albert got him into the next town, the man had devoured nearly the whole sack of oranges. Albert likes to remember how through the providence of God he furnished a table for that hitchhiker in a California wilderness and perhaps saved his life.

Albert liked to surprise people and then see their faces light up as they responded to "a nudge by the Holy Spirit."

Once he responded to such a nudge while speaking to the students at Southwestern Adventist College in Keene, Texas, when he suddenly remembered that the son of a longtime friend attended there. Abruptly he stopped his talk and scanned the audience. Not seeing the boy, he said, "I understand that a son of my old roommate, Julius Knittel, is here. If so, would he please raise his hand." A hand went up. At the end of the meeting, he singled the young Knittel out and put his arm around him as a father. When they shook hands in parting, he pressed a currency note into young Knittel's hand.

At another time an elderly lady, La Vesta Thomas, had just lost her minister-husband, Bob. Now a new pastor would soon be coming to move into the parsonage.

La Vesta had no place to go. She worked into the night so that everything would be ready for the movers, tears flowing freely as she packed things so recently used by her companion.

During the day she spent as much time as she could spare trying to locate another home but finding nothing she could afford. She found a mobile home but discovered she could not pay cash even for it. And considering her financial situation, she felt that monthly payments would be too difficult for her.

Not knowing what else to do, she came back to the parsonage and tried to do some more packing. But anxiety about the future, plus the still-poignant grief over the loss of her husband, so unnerved her that she could only pace the floor in distress. Then she thought of Albert, an old friend of her husband's. Maybe he could suggest something.

La Vesta's tremulous voice and almost incoherent sentences signaled again that "nudge by the Holy Spirit."

"Sure," he said, "go ahead. Secure it with a down payment. Assure them that you'll take it."

Although Albert did not at that point divulge his intentions, La Vesta felt release from her tension and went ahead packing. The next day she gave the people a check for $500 and signed the purchase contract, trusting Albert's word.

A few days later Albert called. "We're sending you a check for the balance you need to buy the house."

"What?"

"Yes," he replied, "we're doing it, and that's it. No back talk. OK?"

"But I'll pay you back."

"No," he said, "we don't want any money paid back from you on this. Mae and I are paying what you can't."

Another table spread in the wilderness.

Loved Kids

Albert never sees a child at the table sitting on a booster chair or a catalog, legs too short to reach the floor, without seeing himself again at that long table in his father's home.

He felt intense sympathy for his own son, wanting to be certain that the boy received the best upbringing.

Even during a meeting with the church completely full of people, Albert the preacher kept track of his son. If he didn't see the youngster beside his mother, he would spot him and say right from the rostrum, "Bob, your mother needs you." And Mother always did.

Albert had taken two summers of teacher training following high school and had taught school one year in North Dakota. But he traces his knowledge of child psychology to his own upbringing, to his reactions and relationships in his boyhood home. He knew loneliness, even though he had brothers and sisters. He had experienced discrimination, intolerance, and injustice.

Albert applied the razor strop when necessary, but afterward would alway put his arm around his son and assure him that he loved him. Even into Bob's college years, Dad Leiske demonstrated his concern for his son in such matters as keeping up the grade-point average and being careful with money. "Watch it," he would write to Bob. "You can do better; you've got the right stuff in you."

During his busy schedule as an evangelist, Albert would notice his son from his office window playing alone outside the tabernacle. Even though pressed for time to get his message ready for the evening meeting, the evangelist would often lean out and call his son over to him.

"Crawl in here," he would say. "You know something? You were born in North Dakota just like your dad. Your mother and I dedicated you to the Lord when you were just a baby. You're special. You belong to Him."

Once Bob wanted a pony, and in this Albert saw his own desire for the white nanny goat of his own boyhood. But a pony just wouldn't fit into their nomadic mode of life. Dad Leiske had to disappoint his boy so often that he feared a rift might develop. He could detect resentment occasionally against their life of constant moving. During his first eight grades Bob never finished one grade in the same school.

The "here we go again" expression on his boy's face whenever Dad had to say "I'm too busy" threw up a red flag. "Could I be sowing the seeds of eventual repudiation of God in my son's mind?" Albert pondered. He dreaded the thought. To prevent this he struggled to make every possible opportunity a time to spend with his boy and to help him, hoping pluses would outweigh the minuses. One day he mentioned to the family a trip he would soon be making to Washington, D.C., to visit President Truman.

"Hey," Bob interjected, "could you do something for me when you're in Washington?"

"Sure, Bob, if I can, I will. What is it?"

"Get a brand-new dollar bill and have the President sign it for me."

Indeed during the interview with the President, Dad remembered his boy back home and asked the chief executive to autograph a new dollar bill. "It's for his birthday," Albert explained, "just turned fourteen."

When Mr. Truman consented to sign Bob's bill, Albert pushed his luck a little farther and got one autographed for a son and one for a daughter of two fellow members of the trip to Washington.

Later when his grandchildren came along, he loved them too. "Old Grandpa Grump sat on a stump," he can still hear his little granddaughters sing as they danced around him, keeping at a safe distance. Then they scampered and squealed as he tore out after them—finally catching them and tickling them till they took back all that they had said.

Children in Pastor Leiske's congregation counted big for him—the "special people" for whom he provided Saturday-night recreation. He wanted them to think of the church as a happy place and of God as loving Father.

Despite static from certain church members when he arranged roller-skating parties, he went ahead with them anyway. And he and Mae joined in the fun, happily letting the kids tag him or her to skate with their pastor or his wife.

During the war years Albert became father to a lot of boys, especially when he pastored the Colorado Springs Church. Many Adventist servicemen were stationed at the base near there for basic training. Some ran into problems. He spent hours in prayer for one boy who had difficulty adjusting to life away from home.

Pastor Albert's interest in the youth of his own congregation spilled over into the community. Why not operate day-care centers—a new concept in those days—for the children of working mothers? It would provide a service, a specialized ministry, for people who needed it. And it could also supply both a source of income for the church and employment for some qualified Adventist ladies.

He even arranged everything, even busing. The church during the week became a world of children, professionally structured to their learning and recreational needs. In Kansas City the enrollment of the church school shot up from 45 to 175 during his stay there, and the church operated the finest day-care center in the city, the Tiny Tot Motel.

Other churches asked Pastor Leiske to help them start day-care centers, the movement spreading throughout the conference, and even to other conferences. Albert promoted

113

the plan as a means to evangelize the community. "The purpose of the Tiny Tot Motel," he said, "is to win boys and girls and fathers and mothers for Christ and His truth." Pastor Leiske found reinforcement for his emphasis on this kind of ministry in a statement in volume 4 of the *Testimonies,* page 423, where Ellen White says that if God had not given her another work, she would have made it the business of her life to care for little children, the "stray lambs." Hundreds of children all over the Midwest and South grew up thinking of Pastor Albert as a father.

"He'll go to bat for you," one said about him. "He provided new blazers for the college band members," remembers another. "He gave me a scholarship for nursing school," a young lady gratefully recalls. "He baptized me when I was fifteen years old, and his preaching still grabs me," said a college youth. "He married us, and we regard him more as our dad than as our preacher," says a couple in Minnesota. "He loved me and put up with my mistakes," Harold Turner, his longtime associate, says with appreciation. "He challenged me as a young man to become a minister, and I'll never forget his encouragement," says Arthur Lickey, another protégé of the Bishop.

So Bob, though an only child, in a broader sense, had brothers and sisters everywhere. And they, like him, still find comfort and support in a bishop who enjoys fun and laughter and wrestling matches and skating parties, one who hopes he'll never grow too old to "be a kid with the kids."

Dreamed Greater Exploits

In February of 1952 Albert and Mae moved to St. Paul, Minnesota, Albert responding to a call to pastor the First Seventh-day Adventist Church there. Just prior to this time, he had pastored in Detroit, and before that in Kansas City, Missouri, and before that in Omaha. In all these places Albert combined his pastoral work with big-city evangelism.

From early morning till late at night Albert packed his days full of activity. One day when pitching a tent, the crew let a rope used for pulling up the main tent slip through the pulley at the top of a thirty-foot pole and fall to the ground. Somehow it had to be threaded back through that pulley. So while others stood around discussing what to do, Albert shinnied up the pole, put the end of the rope through, and slid back down.

"What a guy!" one of his fellow workers said. "That middle initial A in his name must stand for 'Action' or 'Acrobat' or something." "Maybe 'Ape,'" put in another. "Hope I can do that well when I'm fifty." Shortly somebody drew a picture of Albert caricatured as a monkey. Albert laughed with the rest. Nothing mattered as long as the job got done.

"There is a lot of work here," he wrote to his son once, "but that causes joy and happiness for my soul. I love to be busy."

But Albert never allowed his work to deprive him of his hour and a half in the morning for personal devotion and reading. He had a habit of underlining sentences that impressed him and of scribbling notes in the margin, such as "Good counsel" or "Please, Lord, let this happen to me."

One winter morning at home in his study in St. Paul, clad in pajamas and bathrobe, Albert came across a paragraph in Ellen White's *The Desire of Ages* that started him thinking big, challenging thoughts. It said: "Christ showed them [the Jews] that salvation is like the sunshine. It belongs to the whole world."—Pages 306, 307. Albert underlined those words and wrote in the margin, "Certainly enlarges the vision." Then he read in Isaiah 56:7, where God says, "Mine house shall be called an house of prayer for all people," and in Matthew 28:19, "Go ye therefore, and teach all nations."

During that day as the sun shone through the clouds, from time to time Albert reflected on the passages he had read in the morning. Then that evening before going to bed he read another challenging statement by Ellen White (in volume 3 of the *Testimonies,* page 372): "Jesus paid an infinite price to redeem the world, and the race was given into his hands; they became His property." He underlined these words also and wrote in the margin, "Clear enough! It means all men, believers or unbelievers."

"Nations," Albert said to himself, "all nations, all people, and we just dabble around. Instead of having just the deacon and the elder there for prayer meeting, we should have the nations."

He thought of the people he had shut out of his life— people who went to church on a different day or to no church at all. "Christ's property," he mused, "bought by an infinite price."

He thought of Senator Ed Johnson and Governor Ammons and those city mayors—"Christ's property." He thought of the Roman Catholic priest who came to see him once—the first time a priest had ever walked through his door. He thought of Brother O'Dowd and a Baptist minister on Colorado's west slope who once challenged him to a debate. "Whenever I met a preacher, I either had to debate him or argue with him."

His thoughts began to take a different turn, prompted by the passages he had read that day. "It all made quite an impression on me," he recalls. "I found that Christ paid the supreme price for all, not just Seventh-day Adventists. All people, believers or unbelievers, all have become the property of God."

Albert had known for a long time that he could form close personal friendships with members of other religious denominations. He had been able to argue against their positions and yet enjoy being with them and respect them. He did not feel awkward or ill at ease in their presence.

But now in a new way Albert began to feel a love for all these people, seeing them as God's property. "There they are out there," he thought, "millions upon millions of them, making their decision for eternal life or eternal death. The King is coming. We can hear the trumpet sounding, and so many of those people are not ready."

He felt deeply moved by the vision that seemed to pass before him. He thought of a passage in Ellen White's *Testimonies,* volume 6, page 406: "We are to throw aside our narrow, selfish plans, remembering that we have a work of the largest magnitude and highest importance."

"For the first time," Albert recalls, reflecting on his thoughts of that evening, "I discovered that God would rally men of all persuasions to give importance and emphasis to His last-day ministry to a lost world, and that by involving them, He would gather many of them into His true fold."

With these thoughts burned deep into his subconscious, Albert finally went to sleep—and saw a fantastic dream. He seemed to be passing again through his boyhood and youth. His crusading spirit for freedom and democracy and his early abhorrence of intolerance surfaced again. The vow he had made to hit this thing hard if he ever got a chance came ringing back to him.

He saw the cunning enemy of the checkerboard again, making all men intolerant of each other in a game in which everybody loses. And to some extent he even saw himself as having at times played into the enemy's hands.

Albert saw himself in a large conference with a group of clergymen. He recognized them as Roman Catholic priests, Jewish rabbis, and Protestant ministers—Methodists, Presbyterians, Lutherans, Baptists, Episcopalians. . . . "Why not have a public discussion on television," he heard someone say, "and let the people listen in and make their own decisions as to what is truth?"

Finally the group pulled the whole thing together and agreed upon the approach, the charter, the bylaws, everything. Albert joined the others in voting for the plan. Then, somewhat to his consternation, Albert saw himself as moderator of the first panel discussion. The topic he doesn't remember, but he does remember the interchange heating up, almost out of control, till he woke up.

Albert also doesn't remember that he got up in the night and wrote the whole procedure out, just as the group voted it, before going back to sleep. But he knows he did so, because in the morning light he found the thing on his desk in his own handwriting. He hardly knew what to make of it.

"I've got to test this out," Albert decided, "to see if the providence of God is in it or not."

So first he went to see his union conference president that very day, Elder Jere D. Smith. But he purposefully avoided any mention of the dream.

"What would you think," he simply said, "if we had ministers of various denominations discussing our differences on television, as long as it didn't cost us anything? Do you think the denomination would go along with the idea, and would you go along with it?"

"I think it would be a wonderful thing," Elder Smith replied. So Albert had received one clear signal on the positive side.

Next he went to his local conference president, Elder E. R. Osmunson.

"I don't see anything wrong with that at all," the elder said.

"Good," thought Albert, "that makes two."

Next he called the local station, WCCO-TV, asked for an appointment with the manager, and got one.

"I have something interesting. It may have some merit, but I don't want to do anything till I talk to you. What would you think about a program in which ministers of different churches would unite and discuss their differences over television?"

"Just to have them sit together," the manager responded, "would be 75 percent of the success of the show. It would be wonderful."

"Well," Albert came back, "if I can get the ministers together, would we get a time?"

"Sure," he said; "you tell us when you're ready, and we will be ready to go."

Now came the biggest hurdle—convincing the preachers. "Lord," Albert prayed, "if I get the preachers to go along with the plan, I will know that my dream was providentially inspired."

Albert planned his strategy carefully. First, the Baptists, because he knew from his parents' background that they believed in religious freedom. Next, the Methodists, because from Mae he knew them to be liberal and tolerant. Then, the Episcopalians, and so on. Last on Albert's list came the Lutherans.

"As for the Roman Catholics," Albert thought, "they did show up in the dream, but how could they fit into this plan? Could that have been a mistake on the Lord's part?"

The Jews, too, Albert wrote off. "Why bother with them

in an interfaith venture like this?" he reasoned. "They don't even believe in Christ." Nor did he expect the program to continue longer than six or seven months. "As soon as we hit the Sabbath question," he figured, "it will end."

So with his list before him, he fumbled with the dial for a while, trying to tighten up his courage to make the first call. He could hardly believe his ears when he heard Dr. Mahlon Pomeroy say, "Sure, I would be delighted to work with you on television."

"A good start," Albert thought; "now the Methodist." For this slot, Albert had found the name of Dr. Ira Allen. Again a favorable response.

"This is too easy," Albert said, half to himself and half to the Lord. "It's bound to be harder with the Episcopalian." But no, from Dr. Lloyd Gillmett, minister for the Episcopal Church of St. John the Evangelist, he heard the cordial words, "Why, Reverend, I'd be delighted to go in with you on that."

How can this be? Albert marveled. He had no idea that such a reservoir of good will existed among these men. Would his good fortune hold out a little longer? he mused. He pictured a hard-core Lutheran with his clerical collar buttoned behind. "Here we go," he said, dialing Dr. Clifford Nelson of the huge Gloria Dei Lutheran Church in downtown St. Paul, chaplain of the Senate and brother-in-law of a prominent federal judge in Washington, D.C.

Albert nearly fell off his chair when he heard a very pleasant voice responding to his question. "Yes, I would," Dr. Nelson said. "Yes, I would be interested in a round-table discussion on television."

All these preliminaries beckoning Albert to move forward left the newly minted entrepreneur quaking. Debates, yes. Huge evangelistic crowds, no problem. Even defending a man in court could be handled. But television worried him mercilessly. "I was going into a field," he recalls, "absolutely unknown to me."

He walked the floor till midnight. Through Elder Smith he had learned that the General Conference had initially advised against the idea. That little fact bothered him. He learned, too, that in spite of their original favorable replies, at least two of the prospective panel ministers had expressed doubts about the success of the project.

One of them, Dr. Nelson, had evidently even had second thoughts and had called around to some of his fellow clergymen for counsel. News got back to Albert that this man was now feeling skeptical about the plan, particularly, because of the "dream" aspect, which sounded "bizarre" to him.

But Albert remembered his text again: "My thoughts are not your thoughts, neither are your ways my ways, saith the Lord." He felt sure that God's hand had guided in all that had happened.

He thought back to the time in his early ministry when, in his view, the idea of a religious town hall of the air had started—back there when he had been on the griddle in a "cross-examining-the-preacher" night. He remembered how the Lord had given him answers on the spur of the moment and sometimes later in dreams.

He recalled the promise of Acts 2:17 where God says He will pour out His Spirit in the last days: "Your young men shall see visions, and your old men shall dream dreams."

"So we definitely have a scriptural foundation for the plan," Albert reassured himself. And that confidence nerved him to proceed.

First, he felt that the panelists and he, with a few selected other witnesses, should meet and formally sign an agreement. This document would include the charter and the bylaws, all of which Albert had written out in embryo that night following his dream. The project would be officially christened American Religious Town Hall Meeting.

The agreement bound the panelists together in a covenant, spelled out in the document, to sit down before the television cameras and talk over touchy religious differences and problems without rancor or bickering, but with tolerance and a search for understanding.

After the preliminary step, the participants then agreed to go through this formality once again with the klieg lights focused on the ceremony, bringing the event to the attention of the whole world.

That day, December 30, 1952, stands highlighted in Albert's mind with first magnitude brilliance. Among the men who attended the meeting and affixed their signatures to the document were the mayor of St. Paul, the mayor of Minneapolis, and the treasurer of the state of Minnesota.

That night Albert wrote in his diary a simple prayer: "Dear Lord, this year is finishing with the greatest vision You have ever given me. I desire to remain pure and disciplined in harmony with Thy will."

Newspapers the next day used superlatives in publicizing the event. "Perhaps the first time in our nation that such a covenant among five differing clergymen has been drawn up," said *The Anoka Herald,* "one of the most uniquely challenging ideas now before the American public."

It "may have far-reaching consequences," editorialized the *St. Paul Pioneer Press.* "It could admirably supplement the Voice of America and Radio Free Europe in carrying a spiritual message from America to peoples behind the Iron Curtain.

Albert noted with particular satisfaction the words his own union conference president, Elder Jere D. Smith, wrote as he affixed his signature to the inter-faith agreement:

"As I see this group, I am impressed that great good will come of this panel. All of you men are of one accord. It shows bigness. The 265 churches that I represent are all with you, and praying for you in this venture that you are about to launch on television."

Though nothing but applause and approval characterized

the comments that flooded in from everywhere, one little deviation from the dream kept needling Albert's conscience. He had not included the Catholics and the Jews. But six months later the panel itself took the necessary step, adding a spokesman from each of these religious groups. "We saw we had to do this," Albert explains, "in order for the panel to truly speak for religion in America."

"And these groups too," Albert adds, speaking from personal conviction, "are God's property, for whom Christ paid that infinite price." He likes to reflect on how smoothly representatives of these two denominations have fitted into the panel organization. Sentiments expressed by Father Damian Fandal blend with the mood which governs all the discussions: "I have learned in practice something which I suppose I always knew theoretically, namely, that it is entirely possible to have a close personal friendship with, and indeed a deep admiration for, members of other religious denominations, and at the same time disagree with them."

Albert felt a special glow of satisfaction to receive from Father Fandal at a subsequent annual banquet for American Religious Town Hall Meeting representatives the Holy Trinity Medal. The Catholic diocese to which Father Fandal belonged had selected Albert Leiske for this award because of his leading role in civic and religious activities.

Albert felt humbled as well as challenged to be chosen by his fellow panelists as the moderator of the discussions. In the dream he had seen himself in that role, but he hadn't given it much thought since. In the presence of these learned men he felt that certainly one of them would have the necessary experience in television and would logically be chosen. Then Dr. Allen spoke up: "The logical one is the one who founded the organization and has some idea about it."

Albert knew that the only idea he had was the one he had received from God, but he accepted the appointment as

God's doing and prayed for wisdom to measure up to the challenge.

As moderator, Albert remains neutral, a stance difficult for a man of his strong convictions. "But I have to confess," he says, "that, being human, I sometimes tend to influence a panel discussion in the direction of some preconceived view I hold."

Albert introduces the topic and sets the pace of the discussion. He also concludes the discussion period with a brief statement. In between, he deftly guides the interchange with appropriately placed questions and comments, sometimes maintaining order by using his gavel. He often limits his summation comments to a ten-word statement: "Thank you, members of the panel, for your free discussion."

At the first organizational meeting of the panelists, Albert found himself facing a touchy personal problem—what should he be called? The other panelists needed to know how to address him, especially now that he had been chosen moderator. Here he sat among doctors of religion and philosophy, a North Dakota farm boy with not even a college degree and with only the title of "Elder."

He couldn't conscientiously permit the group to call him "Reverend," feeling that this designation belongs to God alone.

He respected the title "Elder," the title the church had vested him with upon his ordination to the gospel ministry. But he found that his colleagues on the panel felt uncomfortable with it, maintaining that in most churches an elder was a layman rather than an ordained clergyman.

For a few tense moments the queston hung in midair. Then Elder Jere Smith, sitting in, proposed a solution: "Let's call him 'Bishop,'"

Albert had never heard a Seventh-day Adventist minister called bishop before, but he listened to Elder Smith's rationale, based on the Bible and the Adventist *Church*

124

Manual. Elder Smith quoted 1 Timothy 3:1: "If any man desire the office of a bishop, he desireth a good work." Then he read a definitive interpretation of the term *bishop* from the 1951 edition of the *Church Manual,* which quoted this same passage in its entirety, but included in parenthesis after the word *bishop* the word *elder.*

So to millions of TV viewers from that day on, Albert became known not only as the moderator of the "Town Hall" but also as Bishop Leiske.

Now that all the nuts and bolts of the organizational structure had been put in place and tightened, Albert felt the euphoric enthusiasm of the group. "When do we start?" they asked.

"Let me call WCCO," Albert suggested, "and see when they have an opening." He remembered that the manager had said, "Tell us when you're ready, and we'll be ready to go."

"And so it came to pass," Albert says, looking back on those historic days, "that the dream began to be fulfilled. The first interfaith telecast appeared on January 10, 1953, at 1:00 p.m."

And Bishop Leiske wrote in his diary: "I knew that God would bring this hour, but I didn't expect it this way. Oh, Lord, I thank You for it all."

Got the Money Somehow

"Sure hope we get a big crowd out," said Bishop Leiske to his colleague, Dr. Ira Allen, as they made their way downtown to one of Philadelphia's largest theaters. Putting into operation a plan to raise money for their new television venture by putting on mock TV panel shows, the five Town Hall panelists had come this night in 1953 to the City of Brotherly Love.

"We ought to," replied Dr. Allen. "The event has been widely advertised, and the theater holds 2000. At one dollar per person a crowd that large could bring $2000."

On stage, though, the usually effervescent Albert simply went limp. He could scarcely count a hundred scattered throughout that cavernous auditorium. To even go on with the show took all the bravado he could muster. He had no heart to make an appeal for money.

"You do it," he nudged Dr. Allen.

The $200 or so they got didn't go very far toward paying the $2500 they owed for their first backdrop. As for getting back to Minneapolis, they had to pay their own way.

Albert had given little consideration to funding the Town Hall. Neither he nor anyone else had thought of including a clause in the agreement about money.

He knew, of course, that the television station would donate the time as a public service, and perhaps that created a psychological blindspot. So when expenses for secretarial help, stamps, typing paper, and telephone calls, etc., began to mount, the newly minted Bishop had to work hard.

Bishop Leiske wrote up a little appeal for publication in his church paper, the *Northern Union Outlook,* and requested the other four panelists to solicit funds from their churches. In addition, contributions began to come in from viewers, but only a trickle.

Albert felt confident, though, that the money would come. "All things are possible with God," he repeated frequently. He knew that God had led him thus far, and he believed He would provide the necessary funds for the future.

His confidence got a much-needed boost one morning when a widow brought him a jar of pennies. The gift seemed symbolic, like Elijah's "little cloud." He recalled George Muller's text, "Open thy mouth wide, and I will fill it" (Psalm 81:10), and he remembered how God had provided funds for Muller's orphanages. Maybe something miraculous will happen for us too, he thought. He would keep praying and trusting—and counting pennies.

The summer of 1954 found Albert trusting and pushing ahead, and planning big things. On his own, he went to Chicago for a meeting with the American Broadcasting Company. He wanted to go national with his Town Hall telecast.

"What about the money?" the company officer had asked. Here again, though the nearly 100 stations would donate the time, the producer would have to foot the filming costs at $700 per telecast.

"Would you agree to a later payment for the first series of five telecasts?" Albert ventured. To his surprise the man agreed, apparently unaware that the entire capital of the American Religious Town Hall Meeting at that moment amounted to no more than $32.

"Who would have thought it?" Albert confided in his fellow panelists as they headed for Chicago the next week for their filming session. "Just another evidence that God is in this thing!" They all agreed.

By December after five filmings, the Town Hall had gone $3500 further into debt. Like Elijah, Albert prayed earnestly. "Dear Lord, we must have relief on our finances. Send Thy power to direct Thy servant to the right place."

"During that very week," Bishop Leiske says, "the answer came." Another miracle happened, only this one far surpassing the jar of pennies.

The Bishop's telephone rang later that day. A cancer patient in the Lutheran Hospital wanted to see him—a man named Martin Kriesel, someone unknown to Albert, but the successful operator of a big business in a nearby suburb.

At the patient's bedside Albert learned that Martin's father had been a Seventh-day Adventist minister. Prompted by warm memories of his boyhood and confidence in his father's prayers, Martin had called Albert, a minister in his father's faith, to pray for his recovery.

"Thank you very much," Martin said as the Bishop got up to go. But a few days later, Albert opened his mail and found a substantial Christmas check from Mr. and Mrs. Martin Kriesel—a contribution to the American Religious Town Hall Meeting. "Thank You, dear Lord," he almost shouted, "You have furnished a table for us in the wilderness *again!*"

As time went on, Bishop Leiske came to know Martin Kriesel as one who enjoyed helping the cause of civil and religious freedom. This businessman followed that first gift with many others, standing out in Albert's estimation as the one man most responsible under God for the financial survival of the American Religious Town Hall Meeting in those early years.

"Gumbo years," Albert describes them, drawing on his farm background for a figure of speech, "those years when it seemed nothing would grow, or at least not very well. I tried everything," the Bishop says, explaining their predicament in more detail. "We wrote to our sponsors and our supporters; we put on mock TV shows in the big cities. But contributions practically stopped coming in. We always operated just one jump ahead of the wolf at our heels." The panelists traveled at their own expense and donated their time. Twice Dr. Allen signed notes so the group could borrow money and keep going.

By April of 1955 the Town Hall had accrued an indebtedness of $8000 with no funds in sight to cover it. Even Albert's faith had become threadbare.

Then to make matters worse, his local conference president called on him, bringing the union conference president with him. They greeted Albert cordially, but Albert could feel icy breath down his neck.

"What about this heavy indebtedness we hear about?" they said. "Do you have any money to pay it off?"

As they went on explaining their concern, Albert hoped they couldn't hear his heart thumping. They feared that since Leiske worked as a minister in the Minnesota Conference of Seventh-day Adventists the creditors might ultimately try to collect from them, making the employing organization responsible for the debts of the employee. At least they didn't want to risk any litigation.

"Brother Leiske," they said, "don't you think that it might be best to close the entire program down before we become too heavily involved financially and embarrassed?"

Albert could see their point of view. But what about his dream? Hadn't God led him?

"Brethren," he said, "I don't know what happened, but I haven't been able to produce the money."

"Well," they concluded, "we'll have to close it down." Albert believes he knows how a convicted prisoner feels upon hearing a judge pronounce the death sentence.

But then all unexpectedly he saw a ray of light, as one of the men started speaking again, saying something about more time. "How much time do you think we ought to give you to see if you can raise the money?" the local conference

129

president asked. Albert thinks the man may have spoken out of turn and later felt his knuckles rapped for asking that question. But it gave Albert his chance to parley.

"I think till July 31," Albert replied. He thought that would give him time to go back into his cave and pray some more, and he could write more letters and visit more people. "I thought of a few millionaires," Albert recalls, "whom I could get in touch with." He watched the men depart, greatly relieved.

Albert worked so hard that summer that when the agreed date of July 31 loomed just ahead it seemed it should still be June. By July 26 the Town Hall had just enough money to keep going day by day, but nothing to apply on the debt.

Then on July 27 he received a letter from a Roman Catholic priest in Oregon, a viewer. "I have inherited fifty cemetery plots in Minneapolis," Albert read, "in the Sunset Cemetery, and I would like to donate them to you." The words seemed like a cruel joke. He tossed it instead into a tray marked "pending"; then he resumed his telephoning and visiting prospective donors.

Next morning the Bishop's secretary called his attention to the priest's letter again, suggesting that the offer might be worth looking into. So Albert called the cemetery and learned that the offer was valid and that the manager of the cemetery valued the lots at $10,500.

"What!" he exclaimed after hanging up, "we need only $8000 to stay alive! And we have two days to go before the deadline." Immediately he phoned the Catholic priest. "We'll be glad to accept your kind offer." Next he phoned his conference president, his hand trembling so much he could hardly hold the receiver. A miracle had pulled the Town Hall out of its first major financial crisis. Still the prankster, Albert couldn't refrain from quipping, "We'll save one of the plots for you, Elder, if you like."

Albert and his fellow panelists knew that they were not out of the woods yet financially. Seeing the need of a firmer operating base, they decided that the first step should be incorporation. On August 8, 1955, they became incorporated as the American Religious Town Hall Meeting. One of the ten articles in the document authorized them as a non-profit corporation to solicit funds, making donor's contributions eligible for income-tax deduction. This article also authorized them to hold property. Another gave them legal permission to sell capital stock not to exceed 100 shares, valued at $250 each. Each share carried with it the right to one vote. Sale of these shares soon provided the Town Hall with a stabilization fund of $25,000.

Article IV provided simply that "duration" of the corporation "shall be perpetual." But four years later economic turbulence again indicated trouble ahead, and the shareholders amended the bylaws to provide for possible dissolution. During the years 1955 to 1968 the panelists saw the specter of bankruptcy looking just ahead of them half the time. Bishop Leiske, almost singlehandedly, kept the corporation alive but nearly killed himself in doing it. Being the president as well as major stockholder, he felt the burden most heavily.

The Bishop had to raise at least $30,000 a year to keep participating stations supplied with kinescopes and to pay operating expenses. This task called for expensive travel and massive correspondence. In 1962 Albert retired from the ministry of his church to give full time to the Town Hall.

"I went on a pension," says the Bishop, "and Mae had her salary coming; that's how we lived." Some years the Leiskes had to subsidize the television budget out of their own meager finances. For example in 1960 the auditor's report showed only $19,681.49 as the total income for the American Religious Town Hall Meeting that year.

"But we kept on going," Albert rejoices. Millions of viewers heard the gospel through the telecasts, which to him made all the exhausting labor and stress abundantly worthwhile.

"We tried many ways of raising money during those hectic days," Bishop Leiske recounts. "We tried to get sponsors, almost succeeding at one point in getting the Kellogg breakfast food company, my 'cornflakes' people to sign on. But in the end we failed."

"Then we tried going into city after city and getting the ministers and the Chamber of Commerce behind it," the Bishop goes on, "but that was hard work."

"Furthermore," Albert says, "we were always in debt." Bills piled up, with never enough money in the bank to keep everything paid up to date. Some months they simply had to pay the creditors who made the biggest fuss and let the rest wait.

None of this struggle had shown up in Albert's dream, and he could not help questioning what had gone wrong. Surely God did not intend His business to be run in this manner.

Finally matters became so critical that the conference officers felt the necessity of stepping in again. They suggested that Albert surrender his ministerial credentials for a time until he could get his financial house in order. Some of his brethren saw him as a wheeler-dealer rather than as an entrepreneur for God. They feared lest reproach should come upon the church.

"Fine," said Albert, seeing the logic in their reasoning and always wanting to cooperate. Inwardly though, he felt a deep hurt and determined to remedy the situation as fast as possible. He and Mae loved the church they had served for almost forty years and wanted nothing to mar its name.

"Please show us Your ways in this matter," they prayed, "those ways that are higher than our ways and so much better. Direct us to a solution to our problems so that we will not bring disgrace upon your cause."

Soon an answer came. Working together with their son, Robert, who by now had become an ordained minister in the Seventh-day Adventist Church, they came up with the idea of sharing their concepts of brotherly love by getting into the health-care field. If handled wisely, they felt, the endeavor could serve the auxiliary function of providing financial support for the Town Hall program.

Acting upon what they felt to be God's prompting, they managed to get enough money together for a down payment on a nursing home in Windsor, Ohio. Almost immediately the Leiskes' hopes proved a reality. This medical facility began channeling funds into the Town Hall operation.

Another opportunity arrived when the mayor of Fargo, North Dakota, a close friend of Albert's, called the Bishop to attend a meeting on urban renewal there. At the meeting Albert suggested that senior citizens displaced by the renovation scheme could be resettled in a complex in some rural area outside Fargo. The idea caught fire and opened the possibility of another facility under Town Hall management. But where would the money come from?

"If it's the Lord's will," he confided in Mae on his return home, "He will provide the means. We'll get the money somehow."

God's answer came in the form of a telephone call from a Roman Catholic priest just outside of Fargo on the Minnesota side. The priest and one of his parishioners, a Mr. John Wimmer, had seen an "American Religious Town Hall Meeting" telecast. So impressed had Mr. Wimmer been that he wanted to make a financial contribution. The priest asked for confirmation, on Mr. Wimmer's behalf, that Town Hall truly qualified as an interfaith organization with a Catholic spokesman on the panel. Upon the Bishop's assurance, Mr. Wimmer mailed a check for $70,000, expressing the hope that "a senior citizens' home might be established in the vicinity of Twin Valley, Minnesota" (just outside of Fargo).

"The hand of God was upon us," Albert reflects. "The Lord was showing us the way, and we had no choice but to follow through."

After the Twin Valley home there came a third facility in Rochester, Minnesota, near the world-famous Mayo Clinic. How many more there would eventually be the Leiskes did not know, but they remained committed to move into any other possibilities the Lord might open up.

Operating the American Religious Town Hall Meeting now became more pleasurable for the Leiskes. Enough money was at last flowing in from the supporting institutions so that bills could be paid on time, with enough left over to start new outreach ministries. The Town Hall added a gospel radio broadcast and a Bible correspondence school. In addition, Albert and Mae, from their personal share of the income, made generous gifts to scholarship funds and church-building projects. They loved to surprise people with well-deserved assist in time of need.

In 1970, responding to an invitation from the Southwestern Union Conference and from the city of Dallas, Texas, the American Religious Town Hall Meeting, Inc., moved to the southland, the Leiskes enjoying the typical Texas-size welcome they received there.

During the 70s new opportunities came for medical ministry. By the end of the decade, the Town Hall owned twelve nursing homes, a retirement home, and three hospitals. What a contrast to those early years of struggle and hardship.

In 1972 came the restoration that meant much to Bishop Leiske—the restoration of his ministerial credentials. To have his fellow Adventist workers express this confidence in him once again brought anew the thrill he experienced when first ordained in 1929. And again he prayed God for grace to measure up to the challenges and responsibilities involved in such a high calling.

Even more recognition came in 1980 at the time of the General Conference session in Dallas, when Seventh-day Adventist President Neal Wilson and other Adventist Church luminaries participated as guest panelists on several telecasts of the "American Religious Town Hall Meeting." His brethren had closed ranks with him again; great peace filled Albert's heart.

Looking back on his money troubles of the 50s and 60s, Albert expresses no regrets. "We started on a shoestring budget," he says, "but the Lord led us through it all."

Shares the Torch

"Bob, your father needs you." The thought struck him oddly. The words sounded like an echo out of the past.

Sitting alone in his St. Paul study, Albert now three score plus, waited for his son to visit. He thought of the many times his son Bob had dutifully responded when he had told him, "Bob, your mother needs you." He remembered also the times he had called to Bob from the study window and Bob had crawled into the tabernacle for a chat.

Now the lad had become a dad himself. And a preacher. Albert thought of the parallel sequence—academy, college, marriage, ordination— that both men had followed. He remembered when Bob had begun to take an active interest in the Town Hall, particularly how he had shared the stress of financial problems which Dad Leiske had struggled with in the late 50s and early 60s. Bob had been the one who came up with the idea of going into the health-care field.

Bob had been along one day when the Bishop and E. R. Colson, treasurer of the Town Hall, went shopping in St. Paul for a new desk needed by the new treasurer.

"We'll take this one. Please charge it."

After running a credit check, the clerk came back and said, "I'm terribly sorry, but your rating is so miserable we can't extend any credit to you."

"I knew that our credit rating was low," the Bishop said, "but if I had known what your attitude would be, I would have gone across the street to your competitor."

"Let me check this again," the merchant replied. In a few minutes he returned and said, "We have changed our position. Please take the desk."

After the treasurer and the Bishop left the store and drove back to the office, Bob recalls that Pastor Colson shook his head and said, "I have traveled all over the world in Seventh-day Adventist mission work, but never before have I heard any man use such a negative position as did A. A. Leiske and turn it into a successful appeal."

The Town Hall Board had asked Bob to administer the Twin Valley nursing home and then to oversee the newly built retirement Town Hall Estate in Rochester. Later, when the Town Hall headquarters moved to Dallas, the board voted Bob vice-president. Finally in 1974 Bob was promoted to president of the corporation. This had been one of Bishop Leiske's goals—that he would have a son who would grow up and take over from him when the time came.

At this point Bob entered the room, and the Bishop felt a glow of satisfaction and a sense of support from the presence of the younger man, his boy, now the president of the corporation.

"Son," he said, "I need to talk over some things with you. Time is running out on me, and there's a lot of unfinished business. Let's spend a little time together, just as we used to, back there when you were a boy."

"Remember, Son, how I tried every device possible to get the crowds to come to the meetings?"

"Yes," said Bob, "always the greatest and most important goal for you remained that one thing—to reach as many as possible with the gospel of Jesus Christ. You always walked fast and talked fast, as if even then you felt time racing against you. I remember I had a hard job keeping up with you. Still do."

"Prejudice kept a lot of people from coming," the Bishop said. "Remember that? Or maybe that complicating factor never entered your mind back than. Intolerance. It weighed on my mind a lot. People would shut themselves out of God's kingdom by refusing to listen and dialogue. Some even tried to shut me up—and would have if they could have had their way."

"That's how your crusade against intolerance got its start, didn't it?" Bob said. "You wanted to build bridges of understanding to people. Right?"

"Yes, and I found many of them willing to meet me halfway, even more than halfway, if I would open my mind to them. Some of them saw us Adventists as self-righteous and clannish. They felt uncomfortable in our presence. I wanted to change that. I wanted to bring our denomination into a more cordial relationship with the others. I thought if they liked us better, they would be more willing to listen to us. My whole thought was focused on winning souls for Christ, the more the better.

"So, then, you dreamed up this Town Hall thing?"

"God gave me that dream, Son. And it has all worked out beautifully. See what we have today. Look at what has happened during the past thirty years with the Town Hall. It fulfills the challenge of reaching the millions, particularly those whose minds have been closed against listening to a strictly Adventist program. The differences in theology may be provocative, but that very factor prompts many into further inquiry and study. Bob, this program is one of the things I wanted to talk to you about."

"Dad, you're concerned about the future of the telecast, aren't you? You want to make sure your dream doesn't turn into some kind of nightmare later on."

"Our goal has been to get this telecast on every station in the nation, and we haven't achieved that by far. To achieve this goal would require a budget of around $150,000 a week. We have a long way to go, because our budget now would cover only about a fifth of that. That's a big part of the unfinished business which you and your associates must complete."

"Dad, do you realize that a big part of that $30,000 or so a week we are now putting out comes from profits on our health-care business? Are you saying we need to increase the number of nursing homes now operated by the Town Hall organization—maybe double or triple the number?"

"That could be an auxiliary goal, Bob, and a worthy one, provided you keep in mind that the thrust of it all must be to preach the gospel and win souls. It's big business for Christ's kingdom. It's not just big business per se."

"We have twelve nursing homes right now and a retirement center," Bob reminded his dad, "plus three hospitals. So to reach the goal you have in mind of blanketing the nation with the Town Hall telecast, we would need at least seventy-five more. Is that what you're trying to tell me?"

"As the hand of Providence opens doors, walk into them," replied the Bishop. "Make sure the Lord is leading. This American dream became a reality through faith and the blessing of God, and its growth depends wholly on His miracle-working power. Never get the idea it is something you can accomplish apart from Him. As long as God permits me to continue, I will devote my whole time to expanding the program so that it can be seen everywhere in the United States. I look forward to what God will do for us and with us."

"You are right, Dad," said Bob. "God still has a great work for you and us to do, and His protection and guidance in the past should give us confidence for moving ahead into the future. The challenges that face us stagger the imagination, but if we walk together in a common effort without compromising principle, we can meet them successfully."

"What a wonderful thing it would be," Dad came in again, "if our Catholic friends across the nation could learn to know Adventists as well as Father Damian Fandal of the Town Hall panel has. He thinks a lot of you, Bob. Through you and others connected with the telecast he has come to know and respect Seventh-day Adventists. He finds it possible now, he tells me, to have a close personal friendship for members of other religious denominations, despite the disagreements in doctrine."

"Have you any idea, Dad," Bob asked, "how many students have enrolled in the Town Hall Family Bible School and are currently studying the correspondence lessons? Nearly a thousand are studying these lessons all the time. A student wrote in the other day saying that the Bible had become a new book to him since studyng the lessons. In fact, he said following biblical principles had now become a way of life to him."

"What about our plans for 'Youth City, U.S.A.'? Any progress on that? You know how I feel about kids and how special this project has been to me."

"Still in the planning stages, Dad. But we're determined to provide a rehabilitation facility for wayward boys and girls. Hope you live to see this dream realized. It will include special provisions for young people to learn toleration and democratic process through actual participation as mayor, city council members, and other civil servants."

"That focus on people appeals to me a great deal," the Bishop responded, "more than buildings or income or anything else. And by the way, make sure this focus is maintained in all our nursing homes too. Our motto is still 'Love Makes the Difference.' Our goal is still to direct patients' minds to the Creator."

"Dad," said Bob, "the Town Hall telecast has added a new dimension to interfaith brotherhood. Your most signal achievement will remain the extensive series of frank, face-to-face public discussions by distinguished spokesmen of differing faiths. The mutual respect and appreciation which have been engendered will continue as an enduring influence for understanding among the churches."

"The credit all goes to God. Humanly speaking, what chance would there have been for me, a simple farm boy from North Dakota, to have done these things?"

"Dad, we want to continue your expansion. We plan to do more in public evangelism. Maybe we can revive the day-care center idea that you began as a pastor. We believe the days ahead are destined to be the most productive, the fastest growing, as well as the most challenging yet for the American Religious Town Hall Meeting."

"Remember, Bob, how we used to go hiking in the mountains of Colorado? Things you have been saying remind me of what we used to see. We would climb to the top of one of those foothills, thinking we had reached our goal. But beyond we would see a higher peak in the distance challenging us. Then rising above that one, another yet higher—maybe a snow-covered one. Always something taller and grander urging the climber on. Remember that?"

"Sure do, Dad. There's always something beyond. Always greater feats to accomplish."

"And now, Bob, let's get moving toward those goals."

The Charter of the American Religious Town Hall Meeting, Inc.

Opening Statement[1]

"My friends: The American Religious Town Hall Meeting, Inc. was created to bring about a better understanding among all people regardless of race or creed, and to preserve our civil and religious freedom in America."

Closing Statement[2]

"And now the Charter: The Charter of the American Religious Town Hall Meeting provides that Roman Catholics, Protestants, Jews, educators, and others may come on this panel and declare their beliefs without hesitancy and the rest of the members of the panel will uphold and guarantee American rights to all who will appear, regardless of race or creed, so that the rest of the world can see that America really believes in civil and religious freedom not only in theory but in reality.

"And now until next week at the same time over the same channel the "American Religious Town Hall Meeting" stands adjourned![3] God bless you all."[4]

---

1. Presented by the Bishop at the beginning of the discussion before the six panelists introduce themselves.

2. After the panelists' summaries and expression of thanks to the TV friends, Bishop Leiske repeats this declaration of Town Hall intent, invitation, and challenge.

3. Here the Bishop strikes his gavel with resounding finality.

4. With both hands raised high, in a benedictive V pattern, the Bishop (with choral segue "God Bless America") accepts the hearty handshakes of the Catholic priest, to his right, and the Jewish rabbi, to his left.